Old & NEW

KATHERINE SORRELL

Old & NEW

COMBINING PAST AND PRESENT
IN CONTEMPORARY HOMES

RYLAND
PETERS
& SMALL

LONDON NEW YORK

First published in the UK in 2002
This compact edition published in 2007
by Ryland Peters & Small
20–21 Jockey's Fields
London WC1R 4BW
www.rylandpeters.com

10 9 8 7 6 5 4 3 2 1

ISBN 978-1-84597-546-3

For this edition:
SENIOR EDITOR Henrietta Heald
DESIGNER Sarah Rock
PICTURE RESEARCH Emily Westlake
PRODUCTION Gemma Moules
PUBLISHING DIRECTOR Alison Starling

CONTENTS

INTRODUCTION

For most of us, decorating is not simply a question of taking an empty room and filling it with brand-new, coordinating furnishings, nor is it a case of inheriting a matching set of priceless antiques. Usually, we're somewhere in the middle – a couple of hand-me-downs here, some chain-store pieces there, perhaps a few things picked up in a junk shop, maybe a special item we've saved up for. And then, of course, our homes are constantly evolving – things wear out or go out of fashion, we get bored with them or they're no longer useful. The old-and-new approach to decorating is a realistic way of tackling these challenges, of celebrating the eclectic mix that surrounds us, and of creating a beautiful, comfortable, characterful response.

Combining old and new – whether in a seamless, harmonious blend, or in a dramatic and surprising juxtaposition – can be done in any room in the home. In this book we have chosen the living room, bedroom, kitchen and bathroom as examples, but there is no reason why you shouldn't extend the principles to a hallway, home office or conservatory.

Wherever you try this approach, there are endless variations. Your scheme may be based on one precious piece surrounded by relatively neutral furnishings, or it may be more diverse, blending all sorts of items together in an intriguing, eye-catching way; it may contrast period architectural detailing with 21st-century sofas and chairs, or place 18th- and 19th-century antiques in an ultra-modern interior; it may take as its starting point a single colour, an ethnic theme or perhaps a retro lighting style. What is certain, however, is that every scheme will be unique and individual.

There are no hard and fast rules when it comes to mixing old and new, but it is worth following the guidelines given on the following pages and drawing inspiration from the illuminating photographs and detailed text. I hope you find this book exciting and informative, and that it prompts you to be bold, imaginative and experimental, creating rooms that are as much a pleasure to be in as to behold.

the
spaces

LIVING SPACES

A mix of old and new pieces can create a living room that is both elegant and eclectic. By pairing new furnishings with older pieces that have developed a pleasing patina of age, you can create a balance in which textures, colours, shapes and styles combine and contrast beautifully, and where subtle harmonies and dramatic differences result in luxurious and relaxing rooms.

THIS PAGE AND OPPOSITE In this welcoming room, plain walls and a bare wooden floor are offset by luxurious accessories such as velvet-covered cushions and a satin and mohair throw; the sofa, though upholstered in classic leather, has simple contemporary lines.

RELAXED MODERN

Combining old and new results in a wonderful mix of the relaxed and the impressive – an interior that is both enjoyable to be in and good to look at. Introducing antique, retro or salvaged furnishings into a modern environment instantly tones down any harsh lines, injects a dash of warmth to cool colours and adds the appealing characteristics of the aged, the worn and the well-loved. The overall look can be as modern as you like, but adding just one or two old pieces provides the necessary air of easy-going repose and mellow pleasure.

The starting point for relaxed modern is always a sense of space: a modern aesthetic can never be achieved if there is too much clutter. Airy, light-filled rooms are ideal, but if your living room is dark and poky there are plenty of ways to lighten it up. Paint the walls a pale, muted colour and use light-coloured flooring – pale wood, carpet or natural matting; you could also consider liming or painting floorboards that are dark or stained. Minimize window treatments, using the simplest of curtains or roller blinds, or perhaps even getting rid of window hangings altogether. Any unattractive or inessential items should be stored out of sight in order to create as much space as possible and ensure that the focus is only on useful or beautiful objects that you love to have around.

LEFT A pair of old armchairs have been re-upholstered in vintage woollen blankets to create an inviting corner for rest and relaxation in a minimalist London loft.

LEFT, ABOVE Modern sofas and chairs accompany a worn wooden storage cupboard. OPPOSITE Classic Le Corbusier armchairs mingle with flea-market pieces in a Paris flat.

OPPOSITE Limed wooden floorboards and a plain, almost austere backdrop give this London loft a pared-down feel, in spite of its period furniture in worn leather and chintzy fabric. The look relies for its effect on lack of clutter and the impact of spots of colour in a light-filled room. BELOW The neutral hues that distinguish this flat are calmly contemporary. The mix includes modern suede-covered pouffes, a classic armchair and, above the radiator, a 1930s Doulton Acid jug. RIGHT Pieces from very different eras are juxtaposed in this relaxed room. The fireplace has an almost medieval feel, while the chairs are modern, covered in hard-wearing denim.

Once the bare bones are in place, you can give some thought to your furnishings. In my view, the one essential in a living room is a capacious sofa or, better still, a pair of them. The sofa can be either old or new; if it is old, make sure it doesn't have any uncomfortable broken springs or worn or torn upholstery. Old sofas, especially in leather, can have a delightfully aged texture, but sometimes re-covering, in a hard-wearing plain cotton, velvet or bouclé, results in a great improvement. Again, pale colours (although impractical if you have children or pets) tend to emphasize a modern aesthetic. You might prefer a couple of armchairs that are big enough to curl up in, or even a chaise longue, which will inevitably add a note of languid elegance to the most pared-down of interiors.

Whatever the size of your living space, plenty of storage is important, so you may find that an antique chest or cupboard or an old cabinet or sideboard makes a useful addition to the mix. A blanket chest or large old trunk, for example,

makes a superb contrast with minimal, modern furnishings, while a lean, low 1950s sideboard would complement the sleek lines and slim styling beloved of modern designers. Or, for an impressive focal point and a distinct change of tone, opt for a more decorative piece such as an antique French armoire with carved detailing, or an old English dresser with distressed paintwork.

When you are buying old or antique furniture, look out for well-made pieces in good-quality materials and simple, understated colours. Natural materials have their own innate integrity, so are always superior to synthetic ones. In a living room, the seductive textures of heavy, grained wood, cool stone, patinated leather and crisp cotton or linen will combine to create a reassuringly timeless atmosphere. Teaming these materials with shades of white, cream, taupe, stone and grey makes for relaxing surroundings, although it's important to include occasional splashes of colour – perhaps some old chintz made into cushion covers, a vintage Welsh blanket used as a sofa throw, some smoky 1970s glassware or a bold 1950s block-print poster. In general, it's a good idea to limit the number of accessories, but displaying one or two carefully chosen pieces that express your interests

ABOVE The eclectic pieces in this airy Parisian apartment, dating from several different periods, all share a clarity of line and feel of skilled craftsmanship which means that they look just right together.
LEFT If you discover a tatty old sofa in a junk shop, you could take inspiration from the owners of this Dutch home and simply swathe it in cream linen or cotton sheets, tucking them in around the edges. The wrinkles and creases contribute to the easy-going, laid-back look.

or personality, whether they be centuries old or made a few years ago, will result in an appealing effect and an entirely contemporary feel.

Last, but not least, consider the way in which lighting can alter the ambience of your living room. Discreet low-voltage downlighters set into the ceiling are almost invisible, but they cast enough light for reading or writing, and can be used to showcase prized ornaments and pictures. You can supplement these with attractive period fittings that have more character, such as a classic Anglepoise lamp or a simple Edwardian-style silk shade, perhaps with beading around the edge. And don't forget that the soft, flickering glow cast by candles is the most restful and flattering light of all.

When putting together a relaxed contemporary look, it is essential to balance elements that will have a softening and soothing effect with those that are more formal and structured. With the right choices of old and new, your living room will gain character from an enviable mix: the grace of the past with the sophistication of the present.

ABOVE The tranquil atmosphere in this converted church derives from the warm colours of the wooden floor and furniture, and the restful simplicity of the repeated motif of horizontal and vertical lines. Old church chairs sit beside a modern daybed and a robust retro coffee table with chrome legs.
RIGHT Several rugs, a country-style dining table and chairs and a classic Anglepoise lamp soften the industrial ethos of this extension to a converted gasworks.

LEFT **The textural contrast of faux fur adds glamour to a classic armchair.**
LEFT, BELOW **A touch of gold, in the form of an 18th-century French chair, livens up a muted palette.**
RIGHT **A Georgian-style sofa has been plainly upholstered so as not to detract from the elaborately framed mirror. A mid-20th-century chair adds another point of interest**
OPPOSITE **The floor and walls make a neutral backdrop for a strong theme of blue and gold.**

GOLD & GLAMOUR

Whether the aim is to create an interior with plenty of impact or to achieve a feel of subtle luxury, nothing beats the glamour of gold. In small quantities, gold adds understated elegance; in larger quantities, it brings high-voltage opulence and drama.

You need only one splash of gold to make this style work, giving your living room a bold focal point while the rest of the furnishings are quietly complementary. For an eye-catching look, choose a piece that is oversized and ornate. An enormous gilt-framed mirror, for example, could be propped against a white wall for a vivid contrast in colour and texture. To show the piece off to best effect, keep the decorative theme simple – painted floorboards rather than thick carpets; Roman blinds rather than dressy swagged curtains.

If your style isn't quite so minimal, it's possible to mix and match a few pieces that share similar attributes – a curving gilt-legged table, for example, will sit happily alongside another item that has the same

FAR LEFT **The velvet-covered French Art Deco armchairs have a sumptuous feel that complements the lines of the modern coffee table.** LEFT **An antique candelabra fills an empty fireplace to dramatic effect.** BELOW **An all-white room provides an excellent backdrop for glamour. Just add a single oversized, eye-catching piece such as this antique mirror with intricate gilt carving.**

attention-grabbing qualities, such as curvaceous Murano glass or an elaborate antique chandelier. Take care not to go overboard, or the effect could become clumsy rather than covetable.

For a more subtle look, combine textures and colours that give an impression of understated luxury. Choose fabrics such as velvet, silk, faux fur and metallic organza, and shapes that twist and twine in an intricate fashion. Elaborate carving, in small doses, enhances this look, particularly when contrasted with relatively minimal surroundings. Decorative elements such as beading, fringing, patterned rugs and Venetian-glass mirrors have a similar effect. Splashes of deep, rich colour – berry reds, midnight blues or chocolate browns – against a pale background will create an atmosphere of indulgence. Clever touches such as these need not cost a fortune, but will come together to create a living room that possesses dreamy, divine glamour in endless abundance.

ABOVE **The bare white walls, exposed brickwork and white vinyl floor give this loft an industrial aesthetic. But it is furnished almost entirely with mid-20th-century pieces, from the plywood Eames chair of 1946 in the foreground to the 1960s Castigioni-inspired floor lamp. The seating on the left is also 1960s in flavour, while the sideboard and sunburst clock are characteristic of the 1950s. The eclectic** combination is both fresh and appealing. ABOVE LEFT **Its plain, flat front and tapering splayed legs put this sideboard firmly in the 1950s. Objects on display are mid-century, too, but the overall feel is more modern, thanks to the prints on the wall above and the vinyl flooring.** LEFT **Although this 1950s sofa is minimal enough to pass as modern, the two table lamps that flank it are very much of their time.**

RETRO-INSPIRED

Furniture and accessories produced in the mid-20th century have a distinctive energy and optimism all their own. Such pieces – whether celebrated modern classics or unassuming pieces by an anonymous designer – have become increasingly popular in contemporary homes, complementing modern schemes in a way that is attractive, easy-going and full of character.

Mid-century retro style can encompass designs from the 1930s through to the 1970s, but, for a fresh, simple look that is not hard to put together, seek out pieces from the 1950s and early 1960s. Sofas, chairs and sideboards from this era are slimline and clean-cut, often raised off the floor on spindly, splayed legs; colours are fresh and clear; and accessories such as clocks, vases and lamps tend to be quirky and eye-catching in character.

To create a retro-inspired living room requires only one key piece, though many people find that once they have bought a single item

they become fascinated with the period and simply can't stop. A long, lean sofa is a good start – either an expensive version by a well-known designer such as Florence Knoll, a re-edition by a major manufacturer or a lucky junk-shop find that needs re-upholstering. Integrate this into a contemporary room by keeping the surroundings as plain as possible – bare boards, parquet or rush matting are best for floors, while white-painted walls allow the distinctive silhouettes of these pieces to stand out. Sideboards and armchairs from the period are key pieces, too, as are spindly lamps with conical shades. If your living room is large enough to incorporate a dining table, you could offset it with a set of typically 1950s Scandinavian chairs.

Retro pieces will integrate well with modern furnishings in a 21st-century living room, on account of their pared-down, delicate designs. They can also make fabulous statements in period homes, standing out against cornicing, ceiling roses and panelling as unexpected contrasts. More eccentric accessories, as long as they are used with care, introduce splashes of colour and fun. After all, this is a look that doesn't take itself too seriously, but creates a combination of old and new that is fresh, individual and enjoyable to live with.

GLOBAL FUSION

In the same way that combining old and new sets up exciting harmonies and contrasts, mixing pieces from East and West creates similarly intriguing juxtapositions. Whether you introduce modern Chinese-style seating into a period living room, or make ancient Oriental artefacts the focal point of a contemporary loft space, a fusion of global styles from a variety of periods is a unique way to bring character and interest to any home.

This look works best when the decorative scheme is based on intense colours such as crimson, chocolate or indigo, which have the ability to transform a living space into an inviting cocoon.

If you prefer a lighter look, simply use a single element of dramatic colour combined with white, taupe, grey or another neutral shade.

In many Eastern cultures, homes tend to be furnished far more sparsely than in the West and to feature seating that is close to the ground. By

ABOVE AND OPPOSITE **This distinctive modern home in Yorkshire was converted from a chapel dating from 1834. The building retains its original stone pillars and wooden floor. The modern, Oriental-style furniture (above) seems initially to create a** stark contrast, but in fact its simple, angular lines perfectly complement those of the old building. The result is a calm, peaceful space that has been given an injection of warmth and drama by the vivid red cushions that form the seats of the chairs and benches.

removing extraneous furnishings and accessories and choosing low-level seating, you will instantly make a start towards creating a distinctly global look. For impact, choose furniture with strong forms or ethnic designs — an Oriental-style chair with a solid, square shape, perhaps, or an African 'throne'; either would make a striking contrast with European furniture from any era. Juxtapose dark woods, cane, brass and other materials typical of Oriental interiors with 21st-century pine, concrete and stainless steel.

An African sculpture or woven basket, Indian saris made into cushion covers, an antique Turkish kilim used as a wall-hanging — these and similar items can all can be used to introduce an element of the exotic into an interior. When aiming to create a pared-down, zen-like feel in a room, use just one or two favourite pieces; for a more dramatic, opulent and embellished style, combine items old and new from around the globe and create an intriguing interior that has immediate warmth and unabashed personality.

LEFT AND FAR LEFT
This tranquil sitting
room is decorated in
predominantly neutral
tones, with two red-
painted walls that
add vibrancy. The
furniture combines
new and old, East
and West, with
simple, spare shapes
sitting side by side
in a seamless mix.
BELOW LEFT Its simple
sculptural shape,
thrown into relief by
the antique wooden
screen, imparts an
Oriental flavour to
this modern vase.
RIGHT Red-painted
beams create an
Oriental feel in a very
old Paris apartment.
The long, low modern
sofa is complemented
by an antique rustic
chair and coffee table.
A hard floor inset with
an intriguing pattern
of octagonal tiles
completes the mix.

LIVING SPACES: getting it right

• Keep it simple – don't try to cram too much furniture into a living room. When mixing pieces from different periods, you need only a few examples of each.

• When you have one very strong pattern in a room, aim to keep the rest of the furnishings plain, avoiding clashes and allowing the pattern the chance to make a dramatic statement.

• For the lines of furniture to stand out properly, wall treatments should be pale and understated.

• Old chairs, from any era, look marvellous re-upholstered in white or off-white fabric. Alternatively, have loose covers made, for a more informal look.

• Lengths of old fabric can be made into cushion covers. Against a plain backdrop, florals, toiles and 1960s prints look great, adding plenty of character and colour.

• For old pieces to work with new ones, they should have a similar feel. Choose clean-lined, pared-down items, and look for shapes that echo each other, such as gently curving lines or boxy silhouettes.

• Look for good-quality furniture with a timeless style. Robust natural materials and excellence in craftsmanship and design provide common factors that unify different pieces, whatever their age.

• Use colour to achieve a coordinated look. For example, if a piece of wooden furniture is out of harmony with the other elements of your living room, try painting it the same colour as the walls.

• Remember that scale is important. One overscaled piece will make an impact, but avoid mixing lots of large and small pieces in one room, or the effect will be crowded and cluttered.

• Attention to scale is also important when it comes to the details. If a table is average in size but has heavy, square legs, for example, it will look wrong next to a chair of similar proportions with slender, tapering legs.

• To avoid creating visual confusion, keep accessories to a minimum, choosing a few low-key, timeless pieces or just a single bold item.

THIS PAGE Surprising combinations and bold contrasts work well in kitchens. Here, the warmth of old wood offsets the glossy sheen of a stainless-steel pan. RIGHT In perfect condition, dining chairs dating from the 1950s (including a fine set of Cherner dining chairs by Paul Goldman) are grouped around a matching table. Their curving lines and warm tones contrast with a shiny modern work unit.

COOKING & EATING SPACES

The kitchen and dining room offer ample opportunities for pairing the traditional with the contemporary. Modern appliances look good contrasted with old-fashioned implements, while new dining tables can be mixed with old chairs, and fitted units can be offset by quirky period pieces.

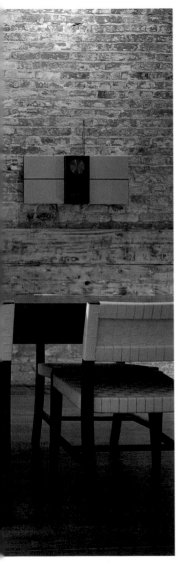

URBAN SOPHISTICATION

Whether you live in a 21st-century loft, a Regency townhouse or an Edwardian mansion block, a casual mix of old and new is an ideal way to soften the hard edges of city living, bringing uncontrived warmth and individuality to an urban dining room or kitchen. Using contemporary furnishings and smart detailing makes it easy to create a sophisticated room that looks impressive and effective, but adding older materials, furniture and accessories will bring the space to life.

The key to this look is texture – every bit as essential an element as colour and form. Contrasting textures can be understated or dramatic, but are always satisfying, bringing an indefinable pleasure and sense of satisfaction to the look and feel of a room. To combine textures requires some careful consideration, but is not excessively difficult. Balance hard against soft, pitted against smooth, matt

LEFT **Classic Arne Jacobsen dining chairs, with wooden frames and slender steel legs, harmonize perfectly with the modern, clean-lined wood and metal dining table.**
RIGHT AND OPPOSITE **Useful open shelving and displays of stylish accessories and foodstuffs help to soften the sleek modernity of angular fitted units.**

against shiny, and the result will be enjoyable and enriching. When using old and new, this comes completely naturally: rugged brick walls against fabric-covered dining chairs; sleek stainless-steel work surfaces against rough plasterwork; a grainy wood dining table with a plastic pendant lamp.

High-quality materials and workmanship are essential for a chic city kitchen or dining room. Rustic finishes won't do; instead, tables, chairs, cupboards and surfaces should be sleek and well turned out, functional but also beautiful. If you are teaming a set of 1950s dining chairs with a new table, for example, ensure that each has its own integrity of form, so that the two looks don't clash.

Finally, add a variety of accessories, perhaps an old industrial-style lamp hanging low over the table, a French enamel sign on the wall, a few contemporary photographs in symmetrical rows or simply a trio of clear glass vases: finishing touches that encapsulate the subtle yet carefully thought-out combinations that make this look so attractive.

LEFT **Lots of light and a generous layout give this kitchen a modern feel, emphasized by the cream fitted units. Traditional elements include a woodworking bench, high stools and a set of old weighing scales.**
ABOVE **Even with new fitted units, this kitchen has a rural feel, thanks to the unusual swan-necked tap and the traditional chequerboard ceramic floor tiles.**

TOP **The timeless quality of this wood-veneer wall cladding is offset by traditional taps, a 1930s clip-on spotlight and an array of good-looking kitchen implements.**
ABOVE RIGHT **The unfitted furniture, scrubbed wooden floorboards and old-fashioned fridge contrast with the white-on-white colour scheme, which gives a minimal-meets-rural effect.**

CONTEMPORARY COUNTRY

A kitchen decorated in country fashion does not have to be traditional or twee. Putting a more contemporary spin on country decor creates an interior that still possesses all the ease and relaxation that makes the country look so appealing, but with a fresh, modern edge that is a delight to live with.

The important thing to remember about the modern country kitchen is that it shouldn't look too fitted. Naturally, you need plenty of storage and work surfaces, but that doesn't mean bland, square units and laminated worktops. Instead, mix modern, fitted elements with an old dresser or butcher's block, a freestanding side table with a low shelf underneath or rows of open shelving.

Some materials are more suitable than others. Knotty pine, for example, tends to look dated and cottagey, although other good-quality woods have a lovely appearance that softens and warms a room. Painted wood gives a country feel without being old-fashioned,

RIGHT **Even in a kitchen with modern fitted units, you can create a rural effect. Simply add open shelving for the display of kettles, teapots or other items, poles or hooks from which to hang saucepans and general implements, and a large table flanked by a set of mismatched chairs.** BELOW **This kitchen features enormous storage cupboards with roomy drawers beneath to contain clutter. A comfortably** large dining table, in sturdy, plain, country style, is matched by a set of simple wooden chairs. The bold contemporary print on the wall counterpoints the other decorative elements in terms of colour and style. OPPOSITE **Fitted and unfitted elements happily coexist in this yellow-themed kitchen, and neat rows of stainless-steel canisters contrast with the rough surface of an old dining table.**

and is an excellent way of disguising any less-than-perfect pieces. Stripped original wooden boards constitute the ideal flooring, while ceramic tiles are the most practical solution for the walls above sinks or work surfaces. Touches of cane and metal are useful additions to the textural mix.

Aim to achieve an overall feeling of light and space. Hang Roman blinds or sheer muslin at the windows to allow in plenty of sunlight, and keep walls and floors plain. Furniture should be simple and sturdy and accessories kept to a minimum, so that each piece adds impact rather than getting lost in clutter. Glass-fronted cupboards are better than ones with solid panels for maintaining an airy openness. Finally, keep displays relatively formal. If you have open shelves, it takes discipline to maintain a tidy appearance, but neat, well-spaced rows of pans, packets or ornaments demonstrate an easy-going country aesthetic combined with a more considered, contemporary style.

OPPOSITE There is a lovely balance here between old wood and steel. The white tiles, while subtle, link the two materials. LEFT Upholstered chairs offset the straight lines and hard metal of a high-tech kitchen. BELOW Although they don't match, these old and new freestanding units possess similar qualities of good looks, durability and sturdiness.

WOOD AND STEEL

A combination of wood and steel almost invariably looks good, the gleaming, reflective nature of metal providing an ideal foil to the more traditional elegance of grained wood. It is a mix that works particularly well in a kitchen, where the necessity for lots of hard, rectangular planes means that it can be all too easy to suffer from monotonous surface textures. The addition of a contrasting material makes all the difference, creating interest, personality and sophisticated appeal.

There are plenty of ways in which to combine wood and steel, the simplest of all being to add wooden chairs to a stainless-steel kitchen or vice versa. This will soften the ambience of a kitchen made entirely from one material, making it both more visually exciting and more comfortable to live with. Equally simple would be to add stainless-steel handles or solid-wood knobs. Alternatively, you could add metal appliances and accessories – fridges, dishwashers, even toasters or lemon squeezers.

GLORIOUS COLOUR

It is all too easy to dismiss antiques as no more than pieces of boring brown furniture. But there is a wealth of ways to bring old, tired items back to life by injections of luscious colour. Kitchens are ideal for this treatment. In living rooms, bedrooms and bathrooms you may want calm, glamour or relaxation, but in the kitchen you can afford a little over-the-top exuberance and uninhibited fun.

Going global is one means of interpreting this look, choosing a fusion of ethnic pieces to create a fun and funky feel. One item may provide a focal point, such as a Moroccan star lantern, a painted Oriental screen or a Gujerati embroidered door-hanging. Or you may prefer to combine a host of items from around the world – Chinese silk tea cosies, Mexican glassware, salvaged French blue-and-white tiles – for an eclectic mix that is rich, exotic and unusual. An alternative is to find retro-style pieces in vivid, unsubtle colourways, from Jacobsenesque dining chairs in bubblegum pink to baby-blue

FAR LEFT, ABOVE AND BELOW The blue-and-white tiles make a marvellous backdrop to a set of patterned ceramic containers and a modern (albeit classically detailed) cooker. The marble-topped breakfast table is an antique find, while the pink chair is a modern re-edition of a classic Arne Jacobsen design. Overall, the look is feminine and light, but the room is practical as well as good-looking.

LEFT AND RIGHT A modern cooker is an efficient addition to a global-style kitchen. The star lantern and turquoise tiles make allusions to Moorish style but the eclectic theme incorporates items as diverse as silk tea cosies from China and doorknobs from India and Africa.

OPPOSITE **Cobalt-blue woodwork and yellow walls set off the table, chairs, cupboard and filing cabinet, all in distressed wood, but the most eye-catching element is crockery – a mix of handmade items by distinguished ceramicist Rupert Spira and cheap high-street pieces.**

LEFT, ABOVE **A collection of old Indian lassi cups makes an unusual display as well as providing storage for kitchen utensils.**
LEFT, BELOW **The sink and mixer tap were both found in salvage yards; their utilitarian looks make a good foil for a child's painting and kitsch ceramics.**

BELOW **Oriental style meets the 1950s in this dining area. The chairs and table have the typical splayed, tapering legs of 1950s design, while the coolie shade of the lamp on the right, combined with the antique screen and chest, introduces a Chinese note to this quirky mix.**

hob kettles or food containers in pretty pastels. Alternatively, simply choose contemporary items, from table linen to crockery, from tiles to lighting, that feature bold, bright shades, mixing them with old tables, chairs and cupboards. If all else fails, you can always add some strongly coloured bowls and plates, a vivid freestanding lamp or some homemade artwork, and paint bland fitted units in dramatic, eye-catching hues.

MID-CENTURY MODERN

LEFT In this open-plan 1970s house, the dining table and chairs, 1950s designs by Charles and Ray Eames, double as a work space. Their metal and plastic finish harmonizes with the modern white kitchen, while the wooden floor, bare window and few accessories are perfectly in tune with the look.
ABOVE This 1960s penthouse flat was refitted in the 1990s. The kitchen itself couldn't be more modern, with plain white and glass-fronted units and stainless steel. The Tulip dining suite, however, is by Eero Saarinen and dates from 1957; although the table's teak top and the chocolate-coloured corduroy chair seats are firmly of their time, the juxtaposition is harmonious.

There is something absolutely distinctive about furniture that was designed in the middle years of the 20th century. Not only is it characterized by classic good looks and timeless appeal, but also it combines effortlessly with modern architecture and furnishings, never looking frumpy or outdated but always fresh and inspiring. A marvellous place to incorporate such mid-century designer pieces in your home is in the kitchen or dining area.

Unfortunately, it is no longer at all likely that you will come across such pieces by chance in jumble sales, skips or house clearances. The popularity of mid-century furniture means that prices are at a premium, but you can still source it through specialist dealers or at auctions. Alternatively, several firms still continue to manufacture pieces to the original designs, while others produce close copies that, to the non-purist, are just as attractive.

If you are planning to incorporate mid-century furniture in a home that is predominantly full of modern pieces, you need to start

by getting rid of clutter and reducing accessories to a minimum. The lines of mid-century furniture pieces are pure and pared down, and to be appreciated at their best they need to be seen without unnecessary distraction.

Walls that are painted white, off-white, taupe, stone or beige provide a subtle background, as do bare wooden floors and windows. The square, regular shapes of contemporary fitted kitchens perfectly complement mid-century furniture, particularly if you pay attention to details such as handles and taps. Lighting should be similarly well thought out; modern recessed spotlights are ideal for this sort of decorative scheme, throwing light exactly where it is required without drawing attention to themselves. Alternatively, a simple

pendant shade, either antique or modern, can be very effective when hung low over a dining table.

Even the most minimal and high tech of contemporary kitchens can look wonderful when combined with mid-century furnishings – sleek stainless-steel or glossy lacquered white units work beautifully with curving plastic, wood or metal. Steer clear of panelled cupboards with fussy detailing or anything that looks remotely rustic – this is a forward-looking, urban style. Accessories, too, such as storage jars, pots and pans, utensils and gadgets, should be selected for their clean lines and clarity of form, in materials such as stainless steel, glass and chrome. If anything hits the wrong note, the solution is simple – hide it in a cupboard and firmly close the door.

ABOVE AND OPPOSITE, LEFT A fitted kitchen in glossy white and stainless steel is home to an array of classic gadgets and some unusual retro-style chairs.

OPPOSITE, RIGHT Paul Goldman designed these Cherner chairs in 1957. Grouped around a matching dining table, they make a striking centrepiece in an up-to-date kitchen with wooden floors and a stainless-steel splashback.

RIGHT A Noguchi paper lantern sails above a table with integrated candle holders, designed by an architectural practice called The Moderns. The plywood and metal Arne Jacobsen chairs complement the materials used in other parts of the room.

COOKING & EATING SPACES: getting it right

• Combine and contrast textures for a feel that is inviting and individual: smooth, shiny stainless steel against rough, bare brickwork, or grained wood against soft cotton upholstery, for example.

• Aim to provide plenty of storage – but not necessarily in the form of fitted modern units. Old dressers, cupboards, butchers' blocks and open shelves are all great additions to the mix.

• Choose efficient modern appliances – cookers, dishwashers, extractors and so on – and mix them with older accessories, or hide them behind specially made cupboard doors.

• The heights of old and new chairs and dining tables may not match up, so take measurements carefully before you rush into making a purchase.

• Create straightforward contrasts between old and new by choosing objects that are well defined and simple in style. If a piece combines more than one style in itself, it will create visual clutter and detract from the overall look.

• Modern kitchens tend to be very square and hard-edged. If this look doesn't suit you, add furniture with curvy outlines (such as old Parisian café chairs) or items that are softer and more giving – perhaps an antique Turkish kilim under a dining table, or a pair of pretty 1950s curtains.

• Be disciplined about open shelves and work surfaces. Having many small items on display is never as effective as a few carefully chosen pieces. One huge antique wooden bowl full of fruit will have much more impact than lots of smaller pieces.

• Old cupboards and dressers can sometimes be massively improved by changing the knobs or handles, or by replacing cracked or warped door panels with fabric, chicken wire or sandblasted or etched glass.

• Plenty of companies now specialize in modern accessories in classic retro designs – juicers, blenders and toasters, to name but a few. Use these to inject instant old-and-new style.

• Keep walls and floors plain, and minimize clutter, so that both antique and modern pieces – such as an English oak dining table combined with a set of 1950s Scandinavian chairs – are shown at their best.

SLEEPING SPACES

The bedroom is a private space where you can be decoratively creative. It's the perfect home for your treasured old and new pieces, but for harmony's sake keep things plain and unassuming, and restrict yourself to one or two dramatic flourishes. Don't cram accessories into the room – clutter is neither restful nor relaxing.

THIS PAGE AND OPPOSITE **Sheer** curtains of a loose metallic weave diffuse natural light as it falls upon a disparate but harmonious collection of pieces The antique mahogany bed, set off by pale lilac walls, highlights the very different texture and colour of a sleek white-leather Mies van der Rohe chair. But the two items share a curvaceous opulence that is set off by the luxurious fur throw and rug.

FAR LEFT **Layers of white bed linen adorn an old iron bed with pretty detailing. The effect is spare and utilitarian but ultimately calming.** LEFT **In another plain and simple bedroom, an old chair sits next to a divan, acting as a bedside table. The white bed linen emphasizes the pared-down purity of the space.**

PURE & SIMPLE

If you want a bedroom that is a relaxed, calming space in which to refresh the senses, you need to start by creating an atmosphere of tranquil simplicity. Fundamental to this effect is a room that is airy rather than cramped, spacious rather than cluttered. Even in the smallest of bedrooms you can achieve this by putting any inessentials out of sight, leaving only the key pieces: a bed, a side table, a lamp, a mirror, a wardrobe and perhaps a chair and one or two accessories. A plain floor is desirable, either scrubbed wood, natural matting or plain carpet with, if necessary, a single rug beside the bed. Walls, too, should be plain and pale, enhancing the sense of space and light. A painting or two will introduce a personal touch, but try to avoid garish colours and heavy frames.

The key item in any sleeping space is, of course, the bed. A modern divan is nicely understated and many have the benefit of a large storage drawer underneath; an antique bed will be prettier, if perhaps not quite so practical. Victorian iron beds, for example, are lovely, and provide a welcome note of decorative detail in a room that is very pared down. The other essentials for bedroom comfort are soft furnishings. Try not to obscure light at the windows, keeping

LEFT **This plain modern divan is adorned with an antique American patchwork quilt in muted pinks. Next to the bed, two old trunks take the place of a bedside table. On the wall above the bed, a modern painting** by American artist Peter Zangrillo acts as an unusual headboard. ABOVE **An efficient lamp is essential for anyone who likes reading in bed. This antique hinged-arm version is beautifully simple yet functional.**

BELOW **When using a mixture of patterns in this type of scheme, make sure they are minimal in style. Basic striped mattress tickings are ideal.** RIGHT **A collection of black-and-white family photos are pegged to a washing line,** and look all the better for this unpretentious treatment. OPPOSITE **A four-poster does not have to be an imposing affair. This one has been made from scaffolding poles, making an industrial contrast to the chintzy bedspread.**

curtains as simple as possible and avoiding fussy pleating and draping, pelmets and tiebacks. Butter muslin makes gorgeous, inexpensive nets, while cotton (perhaps with a very small pattern) or ticking can be transformed into a pair of simple gathered curtains. Wooden colonial-style shutters or a wooden Venetian blind are two simple alternatives.

On the bed, choose white bed linen with the most delicate of trimmings. Then either layer white on white with duvet covers, blankets and throws, or seek out antique textiles that have subtle patterning, either patchwork quilts, satin-edged blankets, floral bedcovers or crochet throws. Ensure that you include a simple but practical bedside table to hold a book, a clock and a vase of flowers. The finishing touches are a directional bedside lamp and dimmable general lighting to create a soft and restful atmosphere.

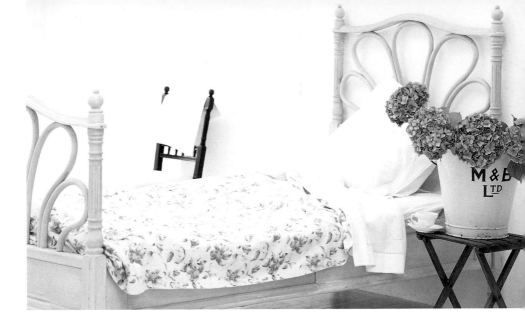

ULTRA-FEMININE BEDROOMS

LEFT **The grandeur of this antique French bed is offset by plain walls and extra-wide wooden floorboards. The feeling of luxury is enhanced by soft pashmina throws and coloured lampshades.**
ABOVE **Vintage florals represent the ultimate in femininity. You can use them as the basis for a simple and pretty guest bedroom. In this example, a dark wooden bedstead has been painted a chalky white and teamed with a chintz bedspread. An armful of hydrangeas in an old enamel bucket adds an attractive finishing touch.**

Interior fashions may be becoming more modern and minimal, pared down and practical, but there will always be a part of most women that cannot resist the opulence of an ultra-feminine bedroom. This is a real boudoir, a sanctuary offering escape from the stresses and realities of the outside world, a haven that possesses comfort and glamour in equal measure. Old and new combine perfectly in this type of bedroom. It is, for example, the ideal setting for a magnificent antique bed, a one-off investment buy that makes a bold statement and captivates the eye. Whether it is a four-poster, an old metal bed or a bed made from intricately carved or prettily painted wood, it is crucial that it has a sumptuous, indulgent feel. Add an old chaise longue, an oversized mirror or a French armoire – any of these pieces will contribute to an evocative, romantic atmosphere.

The other major consideration in a boudoir bedroom is the use of textiles. Even a relatively plain bedroom can be transformed by floral

RIGHT, TOP This unusual antique bed takes pride of place in a modern room, its opulence highlighted by plain white bed linen. It is paired with an antique ottoman and dressing table, the latter topped by a Venetian-glass mirror. A shocking-pink Indian shawl injects a hot splash.

RIGHT, MIDDLE An elegant chaise longue is topped by velvet cushions and a gold sari with metallic-thread embroidery, suggesting the ultimate in sensuality and glamour.

RIGHT, BOTTOM Piles of plump antique quilts and bedcovers are a pretty addition to this look.

OPPOSITE A carved wooden four-poster dominates a simple bedroom with roughly plastered walls and a wooden floor. The bed is clearly the room's focal point, and the other furnishings are deliberately understated to show it off at its best.

fabrics or plenty of patchwork quilts or pashmina throws. The key is not to be restrained: you need layer upon cosy layer to make the room really look the part. Choose pinks, lilacs, soft blues and glamorous golds and bronzes, and remember that texture is important, too – team shiny Chinese silks with embroidered and beaded Indian pieces and soft, fluffy cashmere, keeping an eye open in antiques shops for vintage pieces that can be adapted as throws or cushion covers.

To complete the look, display a generous abundance of accessories. Pile patterned cushions on top of one another. Layer quilts, throws and bedcovers on the ends of beds, even when the beds are not in use. Either hang pretty pictures and ornate mirrors on the walls or prop them up on the floor. And, finally, heap an abundance of flowers in a large container so that their heady scent floats through the room.

LEFT AND OPPOSITE The undulating form of an elegant, curving screen is echoed by that of a modern chaise longue. Panelled walls and a rug add to the feeling of refined luxury.

BELOW In this masculine room, a carefully contrived colour scheme pulls together old (a Bertoia Diamond chair dating from 1952) and new (a Richard Sapper Tizio lamp).

UNDERSTATED ELEGANCE

To enjoy a good night's sleep, we need a comfortable bed and calm surroundings – a muted colour scheme, simple furniture, subtle lighting. All these elements add up to a bedroom that is sophisticated and elegant, where antiques are combined with chic modern pieces to create an atmosphere that promotes rest and relaxation.

If you want to achieve a look of understated elegance, don't emphasize a single exotic item but try to create a natural combination of furniture and accessories that blend into a seamless whole. The bed itself can be relatively ordinary – a divan is fine – but should be dressed in attractive linens with a smart, tailored appearance. Avoid fuss or frills of any kind; instead, take inspiration from Savile Row suiting by introducing narrowly striped or hemstitched sheets.

Enhance the sense of luxury by covering the floor with deep-pile rugs, perhaps with a subtle pattern; you could even hang a rug on the wall for a rich and sumptuous effect – or walls could be panelled

LEFT **This tranquil bedroom bathed in light is enhanced by exotic details. Pieces collected by the owner on her travels, all in neutral colours and made to high standards, have been put together to create an eclectic yet harmonious whole.** RIGHT **The taupe and ivory colour scheme creates a mood of calm contemplation. The oversized headboard, teamed with layers of bed linen in coordinating colours, make a simple divan look impressive, while the cowhide-covered ottoman adds a light-hearted touch.**

with varnished wood veneer reminiscent of an upmarket gentlemen's club. Furnishings should be kept to a minimum, each piece chosen for its quality of materials and manufacture. Junk-shop finds are unlikely to make the grade, but classic designer pieces are perfect, with the emphasis on function as well as aesthetics. A bedside table, a chair or a chaise longue, perhaps a screen to disguise a dressing area, are all that is needed – they could be old or new, English, European or Far Eastern, as long as they demonstrate fine forms and good workmanship.

Lighting is vital to achieving success with this look. Recessed downlighters fitted in the ceiling will give general illumination without unwanted glare or dazzle, while for reading in bed a pair of adjustable lamps is best – either adjusted to an appropriate height on bedside tables or attached to the wall behind and to either side of the bed. Modern lamps are ideal for this purpose, and have the sort of sleek, slimline design that is appropriate to this understated scheme.

Perhaps the most important consideration of all, however, is colour. Avoid bright hues and choose instead naturals and neutrals: white, taupe, ivory, stone, shell, and so on – all of which will enhance the sense of space and light, and result in a calm, considered atmosphere. For a more masculine approach, choose shades of grey, from dove to charcoal, and navy, or even deep reds and greens, resulting in a warm and intimate space that is nevertheless refined, dignified and tasteful.

SLEEPING SPACES: getting it right

• Avoid bedroom clutter by investing in large wardrobes, cupboards and chests of drawers. These could be modern, built-in versions with invisible push-touch hinges or, for a more dramatic and individual statement, antique armoires.

• The bed should be the focal point of the room. If you can afford a beautiful antique, keep the linen simple and understated, so the bed's design can stand out. If you have a modern divan, layer quilts, throws and cushions for a luxurious effect.

• Clever colour schemes can pull a look together, uniting antique and modern pieces. Generally, pale colours such as ivory and taupe are calming and restful, but stronger colours can sometimes be more cosy and inviting. If you have a wonderful bed, you could paint only the wall behind the bed to draw attention to it.

• Keep flooring neutral to provide a plain backdrop that will show off pieces of furniture with interesting shapes and colours to their best advantage.

• A bedside rug is very comforting underfoot. Choose one that's plain or features a subtle pattern that doesn't detract from other furnishings.

• Even if you invest in an antique bed, you should always buy a good-quality new mattress. We spend an average of twenty-five years of our lives in bed, so it's worth ensuring that your bed is not lumpy, too hard or too soft.

• Choose furniture linked by colour, shape or material. The less fussy the decoration and the cleaner the lines, the more likely that old and new pieces will harmonize well.

• Dimmable lights are a good idea for overall illumination. Recessed downlighters in the ceiling will work with an old-and-new scheme because they don't draw any attention to themselves.

• Accessories can add pretty touches to a bedroom scheme, from enamel jugs to chintz-printed bowls, from an old sari used as a bedcover to a Venetian-glass mirror, from an African stool to a tailor's dummy.

• Whether it's a sleek, modern halogen light or a 1930s chrome version, an adjustable bedside lamp is indispensable for easy bedtime reading.

BATHING SPACES

A bathroom should be an oasis – an intimate place for contemplation, pampering and relaxation. Here, a combination of old and new gives a sense of luxury and individuality that will prove the source of endless pleasure. Surprising juxtapositions such as 21st-century taps paired with a 19th-century roll-top bath create a sense of drama, while subtler details provide food for thought and a chance to unwind in idyllic surroundings.

THIS PAGE AND OPPOSITE The sharp, square outline of this huge bath, covered in mosaic tiles (in an appropriate shade of turquoise), is very modern. The effect is tempered by the addition of a pair of antique cross-head taps and, in the background, a cast-iron column radiator. The gently worn patina of these old pieces softens the room and enriches it with a sense of timeless comfort.

LEFT AND OPPOSITE
An old roll-top
bath contrasts
with avant-garde
Philippe Starck
taps and a basin
with an exposed
chrome waste.
RIGHT The pair of
carvings placed
symmetrically in a
triangular chimney
breast are the
focal point of this
fashion designer's
bathroom.
BELOW RIGHT This
bath is simply a
rectangular box
sunk deep into the
floor of an intimate
side room. Tiny
mosaic tiles and a
stone wall provide
plenty of interest.

TOTAL TRANQUILLITY

If you are seeking to create a bathroom that is a haven of tranquillity
and an oasis of calm, there is no better style than one that is pared
down to the bare essentials. With no clutter to distract you from a
long hot soak with essential oils and a candle, this is a room that will
be guaranteed to refresh and revive.

Central to the idea of a tranquil bathroom is a really comfortable
bath – if possible, one that is slightly larger than average and maybe,
if you are lucky, a freestanding one. An Edwardian roll-top bath with
claw feet is perfect, although this type of bath is not as easy to find
now as it used to be. However, some manufacturers make high-
quality reproductions that look just as attractive as the originals. An
ordinary built-in bath can be made to look more attractive with the
addition of an interesting side panel, perhaps made of varnished or
painted marine ply or covered with tiny mosaic tiles.

LEFT **Choose plain accessories for a restful scheme.**
RIGHT **White-on-white tiling creates a a room that is clean, simple and serene.**
BELOW LEFT **A massive iroko wood screen separates a bathroom from the master bedroom and acts as a headboard for the bed. The rich tones of the wood offer a warm contrast to the blue mosaic tiles that line the bathing area beyond.**
OPPOSITE **An expanse of frosted glass creates an ethereal impression that is emphasized by pale colours and clean lines. Fluffy white towels add a cosy, tactile touch.**

For an intriguing juxtaposition of old and new, combine a restored antique bath or sink with minimal, ultra-modern taps and shower attachments. You could also offset a sleek new sink by setting it against a roughly plastered wall, or hang an old Venetian-glass or wood-framed mirror above a thoroughly modern glass basin. While it is advisable to keep other furnishings to a minimum in a bathroom, if the space is available you may wish to add an antique chest or cupboard for storing towels and toiletries, or a chair or stool on which to place discarded clothes, books and other items.

Most important of all, choose colours that are muted, subtle and sophisticated. A single wall painted in turquoise or deep red will look wonderfully effective, as will wooden panelling and one or two pieces of freestanding furniture made from dark wood, but the overall effect should be light and airy, to create as peaceful an atmosphere as you possibly can.

LEFT Antique copper baths, with their rich colour and generous curves, are the ideal focal point for an old-and-new room. RIGHT A series of framed architectural prints create the sort of traditional 'print-room' effect more usually seen in a living or dining space. BELOW RIGHT Since they share a similar design style, the varied elements of this bathroom are brought together to opulent rather than discordant effect. OPPOSITE The lovely antique bath and shower attachment makes a wonderful contrast with the ultra-modern floor-to-ceiling windows.

OPULENT INDULGENCE

If you want a bathroom that makes a statement – a dramatic space in which you will feel invigorated and inspired – aim to create a high-impact look that combines old and new with imagination and flair, resulting in drop-dead gorgeousness and over-the-top glamour.

The secret to achieving this wow factor is often to include one extraordinary item – whether it is an unusual bath, an impressive mirror or even an incredible view. Specialists in antique sanitaryware sometimes have amazing old French baths, huge shower roses and oversized, patterned sinks – but these items do not come cheap. A less expensive alternative is to use plain modern fittings and combine them with strong paint colours and interesting freestanding pieces, be they chairs, side tables, chests or cabinets.

Another way of making a statement without going to enormous expense is to use coloured or patterned tiles to cover the floor or the walls. These could be richly coloured Moroccan tiles, delicate mosaics or antique Victorian examples found at a salvage yard.

Since this bathroom look is intended to be ornate and sumptuous, look for pieces with elaborate, decorative shapes and forms – bring on the gilt, the carving, the rich embellishments. For a unified look, however, keep to a coherent colour scheme, and make sure that your furnishings either all date from the same period or clearly share a similar decorative intent.

TOP **This bright and airy city bathroom has a dash of glamour in the shape of a lovely antique giltwood mirror hung above the washbasin.** ABOVE **A large silver-coloured mirror, a sleek wall of custom-made** cupboards and sophisticated lighting make this bathroom a luxurious space in which to unwind. RIGHT **Unusual freestanding pieces of furniture can add plenty of personality to a bathroom.** OPPOSITE **Plain walls and flooring provide the perfect backdrop for a large Victorian clawfoot bath, a wrought-iron trolley and a pretty Venetian-glass mirror, all of which convey a feeling of opulence.**

OPPOSITE White-painted beams and wooden walls give this bathroom a simple, spare country feel that is emphasized by the large square bath and the floor of terracotta tiles. LEFT Old oak beams and painted wooden boards are appealingly down-to-earth. The tiled splashback adds a dash of colour and pattern. BELOW Old wood and bright stripes are a bold mixture. The dramatic paintwork draws attention away from the bland modern toilet.

RURAL RETREAT

The country-style bathroom is simple and functional, uncomplicated and unpretentious, with a leisurely yet slightly utilitarian feel. It offers a welcome retreat from modern life – somewhere to relax and unwind.

Natural materials are at the heart of this look, and the most essential material of all is wood. If you are fortunate enough to have a bathroom with a beamed ceiling, leave the wood bare or paint it white, duck-egg blue or sunny yellow. Tongue-and-groove panelling introduces a country flavour to any room while providing a durable and practical wall covering, especially when coated with paint specially formulated for bathrooms. Stripped floorboards will also strike the right note, although in a colder climate you might want to add warm rag rugs or cotton runners underfoot. Accessories in other unassuming materials, such as enamelled buckets, straw or wicker baskets and hand-painted ceramic tiles will help to create an effect of simple and uncontrived rusticity.

ABOVE **In a newly converted attic bathroom, an antique dressing table and rustic stool are placed below a window to make the most of natural light.**
ABOVE RIGHT **A fitted wardrobe covering an entire wall holds all sorts of bathroom items. The warmth of the wood adds to the cosy atmosphere.**
OPPOSITE **Natural light enhances the peaceful feel of this country-style bathroom. The runners make it warm underfoot.**

The idea of returning to nature is an appealing one, but not many of us could survive happily without the comforts of modern life. In a country-style bathroom, it is essential to strike a balance between practicality and prettiness. Choose modern fittings such as reproduction roll-top baths or chunky taps that function well while possessing old-fashioned good looks. If chosen carefully, power showers, heated towel rails and chic lighting all have their place in a rural retreat, making for a bathroom that's enjoyably easy to spend time in – heart-warming, welcoming and homely.

BATHING SPACES: getting it right

• Old freestanding pieces bring character to a fitted bathroom, but leave plenty of floor area clear to create a spacious, airy feel.

• If you are on a budget, install cheap white modern sanitaryware. Search junk shops and markets for freestanding furniture and pretty accessories that will make an impact against the modern fittings.

• If necessary, you can have old baths re-enamelled so that their surfaces are clean, new and pleasant to bathe in.

• When buying old fittings, check that all dimensions make the items suitable to take modern plumbing.

• If you want to install a reclaimed cast-iron bath, first make sure that your floor is strong enough to support the combined weight of the bath, the water and a bather.

• Use tiles to unify a scheme. Plain white tiles make an ideal background for opulent antiques, while coloured and hand-painted tiles (whether old or new) can be teamed with less exotic modern fittings to add atmosphere.

the elements

THIS PAGE AND OPPOSITE
Some antique furniture can
appear heavy and dark – hard
to fit into a modern home. But
using pale cotton or canvas

loose covers or cushions, or
even simply swathing fabric
around a chair, will update a
piece and imbue it with an air
of lightness and modernity.

FURNITURE

The building blocks of any home, pieces of furniture comes in many guises, and a combination of old and new can be both effective and appealing. You may simply wish to add an antique stool to an otherwise contemporary sitting room, or you may prefer to create an eclectic mix that brings together pieces from different periods in an inspiring way. Whatever your aim, carefully chosen chairs and tables, chests and cupboards can underline connections and contrasts between one era and another.

SEATING

Chairs play an important role in the old-and-new look. From a battered leather club chair to a 21st-century steel one, from a bentwood Thonet chair to a 1950s-style dining chair upholstered in zebra skin, these pieces are frequently cheap and easy to find, while being simple to move around, to re-upholster or cover, or to accessorize with throws or cushions. It is easy to make an antique chair work in a contemporary room, or a new chair in a period setting.

Sometimes it is the clash of cultures that makes mixing old and new particularly interesting, and installing a chair from one period in a home from another period can be a quick and easy way to achieve this effect. In a Victorian, Georgian or older house that features panelling, cornicing, brickwork or beams, you could introduce a very different element in the shape of a Danish mid-20th-century chair, a 1960s plastic stool or a 21st-century clear acrylic chair. The juxtaposition of the two aesthetics will be striking: setting plastic against rough plasterwork or steel against wood panelling is surprisingly effective. The key to making the look work is to keep other furnishings

OPPOSITE, CLOCKWISE FROM LEFT **Lofty glass-panelled doors and a stone floor provide a clean backdrop for a 1970 Rocker chair by Marc Held. A burnished-leather club chair is in harmony with modern stripped floorboards and plain white walls. White cotton cushion covers allow an old cane chair to look at home in a minimalist setting,** despite its traditional style. The fabric sets up a contrast with the armchair's carved wooden detailing.
ABOVE LEFT A capacious antique armchair has been re-upholstered in tweed, adding a spin to a timeless design.
LEFT The lightness of the wire Bertoia chair makes it a versatile choice – it has minimal impact but great flair.

to a minimum and avoid garish or distracting patterns or over-complex forms. Trying too hard will only result in confusion, but allow the pieces to speak for themselves and they will interact with their surroundings in a most positive way.

If your home is modern in style, an antique chair can add a note of old-fashioned comfort, a dash of opulence or an element of sophisticated chic. Leather club chairs, buttoned armchairs upholstered in checks or tweed, Louis-style carved wooden chairs or Victorian cane chairs all have marvellous character and bring a room to life. Such elements will prevent a contemporary home from becoming bland, while lofts that are dominated by materials such as glass and steel frequently benefit

from the addition of an unexpected piece that contrasts with their sleek architectural detailing.

Junk shops, second-hand shops, auctions and the less expensive antiques dealers are all good sources for old chairs. Sometimes they may be a little battered and tired – this may simply add to their appeal, or you may prefer to have them repaired or given a new coat of paint, stain or varnish. Often the most unpromising piece can blossom into a beauty when painted the right colour. Re-upholstering an old chair also makes a huge difference to its appearance: using a plain, heavy off-white cotton or canvas adds simplicity and allows most pieces to fit into most rooms. Alternatively, you could be daring and choose a

LEFT Marco Zanuso's Lady armchair looks remarkably modern despite dating back to 1951. Here, its streamlined shape works well in a light-filled contemporary interior that reveals a passion for mid-20th-century styling.
RIGHT An Ernest Race Antelope chair, designed in 1951 for the Festival of Britain, makes a bold statement in a modern home.

RIGHT **Verner Panton's S chair of 1968 looks positively futuristic, even in a modern interior.**
BELOW FAR RIGHT **This distinctive chair by Robin Day has the simple square lines and clean-cut character that would work well today in a minimalist setting.**

bold 'statement' fabric that contrasts with a more traditional shape in an exciting and dynamic way. Loose covers are a less expensive option.

Bear in mind that old chairs can be found in the most disparate places, from skips to school sales, from garden furniture shops to architectural salvage companies. Department stores can provide straightforward, inexpensive contemporary pieces, or you can go to a specialist for a modern-classic designer chair that will do serious damage to your bank balance. An interesting chair, of whatever type or style, can single-handedly create an impressive old-and-new look that will set the tone for the rest of your scheme.

ABOVE **These old folding church chairs in dark wood have a timeless solidity and dignity. They are guaranteed to add depth and character to any room as well as providing useful addition seating.**
LEFT **In this light, bright room, a mix of seating creates an informal dining area. Although the chairs (and bench) may represent a wide variety of styles, they share a visual coherence – all are simple to the point of being rustic, without any ornamentation.**

RIGHT AND BELOW
Old garden seating works particularly well when used indoors. Repainting it adds a certain sophistication, so it doesn't look too out of place when seen next to conventional furnishings.

LEFT The rich carving that adorns this ancient chest is in strong contrast to the simply framed modern photographs displayed above it.

RIGHT Former office furniture can often be adapted in an ingenious fashion for domestic use. Here, the narrow drawers of an old-fashioned wooden architect's plan chest are useful for storing papers and drawings, and would look good in both a formal and an informal setting.

FAR RIGHT The mix of styles in this home office is unobtrusive because each item of furniture has a pleasing simplicity. The former school lockers are used for the storage of files, computer discs and so on. The lack of clutter and the clean white floor and walls create an overall effect that is quirky rather than junky.

WARDROBES, CHESTS & OTHER STORAGE

Every home requires plenty of storage, and mixing old and new pieces is a clever way in which to blend practicality with aesthetic appeal. Whether you are considering a living room or bedroom, a kitchen or bathroom, a hallway or a home office, chests, cabinets, dressers, wardrobes, armoires and sideboards, both antique and modern, can play a useful role in daily life, while also making an invaluable contribution to a decorative scheme.

An instant way of adding interest to a modern home is to provide a bold feature in the form of an oversized period storage piece. It may be carved or painted, or adorned by an imposing, scrolling outline. A Renaissance chest, for example, a

19th-century Italian wardrobe, an Indian cupboard, a decorative French armoire, a lacquered Oriental cabinet – any of these would create an impact when set against plain painted walls, exposed concrete, bare brickwork or metal beams. Equally, any of these would provide storage for all sorts of items, from wine glasses to towels, from drinks to office equipment. Statement pieces such as these tend to be inherited (if you are lucky) or found at the grander antique shops and auction houses.

Less imposing (and less expensive) pieces can also enrich a contemporary room, albeit in a more understated way: for example, country-style dressers, utilitarian filing cabinets or simple pine

LEFT In an airy modern room, the beautiful grain of an old wooden plan chest adds character and individuality. Its large top makes a wonderful surface for attractive displays.

OPPOSITE, ABOVE LEFT Wall-hung cupboards are a useful way of putting clutter out of sight. Country-style pieces such as this one are relatively easy to find.

OPPOSITE, BELOW LEFT Distressed paintwork adds to the character of old wooden pieces.

OPPOSITE, RIGHT This mirrored armoire has moved from the bedroom to the living room, where it now serves as an unusual drinks cabinet.

blanket boxes can harmonize well with more modern pieces. Such items can sometimes be picked up at house and office clearance sales or in second-hand shops and they tend to be relatively good value, particularly if they need some minor renovation in the form of sanding or painting.

In a period home, it is also possible to combine old and new by introducing brand-new storage pieces. Elaborate cornicing, ceiling roses, skirting and panelling can be offset with plain, pared-down cupboards or units in wood veneer or metal, their sleek surfaces contrasting quietly with the decorative nature of their surroundings. A modern designer sideboard could easily become the focal point of a Georgian dining room, for example, while a minimal Scandinavian

LEFT Dramatic lighting shows off the wonderful features of this antique Chinese scholar's desk. Set within a modern brushed-glass screen, it is the focal point of a minimalist loft. BELOW The colour and patina of a recently painted wall superbly offsets those of the 1960s cabinet set in front of it. BELOW LEFT AND OPPOSITE Retro pieces, especially those dating from the 1950s, have a distinctive style that gives them great character. They tend to be free of panelling, carving and elaborate outlines, featuring instead tapering legs, plain doors and a long, low outline that immediately indicates their origin. They offer ideal storage for narrow rooms and small spaces, and frequently provide very convenient surfaces for the display of lamps, vases, bowls and other objects.

chest of drawers would look at home in a bedroom with a Shaker four-poster bed. Whether you are in a bargain chain store or a chic boutique offering the very latest European designs, keep your eyes open for storage items that would work well in your living space. If designer pieces are out of your price range, bear in mind that some shops have regular end-of-line sales offering substantial discounts, and it is also worth looking for bargains on the internet.

An imaginative approach will reap rewards. After all, at the heart of the old-and-new look is a willingness to embrace experimentation and the unexpected. So, a 1940s polished-steel office filing cabinet would be a quirky place to store shampoo, soap and other essentials in a bathroom, while a carved wooden armoire could double as a fabulous drinks cabinet in the living room; a carved oak coffer might hold umbrellas and Wellington boots in the hallway, or a Tibetan cabinet could conceal a collection of shoes in a spare bedroom. Old pieces can often be adapted to modern uses (although it

is unwise to make changes to valuable antiques of any type). If you drill a small hole in the back of an old dresser, for example, you can pass an electric lead through the hole to a socket, transforming the dresser into storage for a television, a DVD player or a hi-fi system. If necessary, you can even add extra shelving for storing DVDs, videos or CDs.

Sometimes, no adaptation is required. You can easily make a guest room that doubles as a home office appear more welcoming by concealing files, stationery or even computer equipment inside an antique wooden armoire or cabinet. Failing that, stack the office paraphernalia on simple shelves, which can then be concealed by an antique curtain or a length of vintage fabric.

LEFT A lovely old oak refectory table is given more impact by its juxtaposition with a set of classic 3107 dining chairs designed by Arne Jacobsen in 1955.

OPPOSITE, ABOVE LEFT A new wooden dining table is surrounded by old-fashioned rush-seated chairs in front of a Victorian fireplace to create a relaxed dining room.

OPPOSITE, ABOVE RIGHT In an almost-empty room, a low modern table offers an ideal surface for a display of antique Oriental artefacts.

OPPOSITE, BELOW This simple old console table, painted white, is an understated piece that goes well with modern side chairs and the pared-down, airy aesthetic of a contemporary living room.

TABLES

One of the most exciting opportunities for unusual juxtapositions of old and new is offered by a dining table and its accompanying chairs. A pleasing effect can be achieved by setting up a contrast between the strength and solidity of a wooden table with a scoured and scrubbed surface and new chairs in smooth plywood, shiny plastic or sleek steel. Alternatively, combine a chic modern table with old chairs. This look will be even more effective if the chairs don't match, so you can have fun seeking them out in all sorts of places, from school sales to junk shops and even in skips.

Side tables, console tables, bedside tables and, of course, coffee tables can also be essential elements in this type of scheme. An enormous coffee table made from reclaimed railway sleepers or an old Indian door would look fabulous in a minimalist modern living room, for example, while a slim, contemporary console table, made from pale wood, metal or sandblasted glass, would be an inspired addition to a traditional hallway.

LIGHTING

If you are looking for just one showstopping piece to bring dramatic contrast to a contemporary room, the answer may be a sparkling chandelier, a spindly 1950s floor lamp or an oversized 1960s plastic lampshade. Antique lighting makes the perfect accessory to modern furnishings, counterpointing clean lines with ornate or over-the-top details, and cool colours with vivid tones.

THIS PAGE AND OPPOSITE Antique chandeliers (and contemporary reproductions) possess a unique attention-grabbing appeal. Their sparkly droplets and twining shapes catch the eye and contrast well with minimal modern furnishings and accessories.

GLAMOROUS

Planning a lighting scheme is crucial when decorating a home, and functional lighting should be installed before any other elements. However, if you want to introduce a dash of glorious glamour in the shape of decorative lighting, then it is best left until last. This means that you can forage around in junk shops or at car-boot sales or jumble sales and visit antiques dealers until you find the perfect piece to complement your room.

Perhaps the most flamboyant type of glamorous lighting is the antique chandelier, made from wrought metal and faceted glass drops (designed to maximize sparkle) that are either coloured or clear. Chandeliers range in style from extremely ornate to relatively simple and, although some cost a fortune, it is still possible to find examples that aren't too expensive. But there are all sorts of alternatives, too, ranging from traditional metal candelabra that can provide a superb contrast to a contemporary living room, to modern, Moorish-style glass lanterns that would look fabulous over a traditional-style dining table. In general, look out for intricate shapes, luxurious materials and intense colours, and the results won't fail to dazzle and delight.

ABOVE LEFT AND ABOVE **The aptly named Fun chandelier, designed in 1964 by Verner Panton, is a deluge of sparkling shells and glittering metal. It would be a sensational focal point in any room.** OPPOSITE **Nothing is more glamorous than an antique** glass chandelier. The larger ones make wonderful centrepieces, and look very striking juxtaposed with contemporary furnishings, while less obvious examples, in the form of wall lights or table lamps, still draw the eye and add sparkle to any living space.

RETRO

Lighting from the period from the 1930s to the 1970s tends to fall into two design styles: the practical and the decorative. The former type will often have adjustable supports or a flexible stem, so that illumination can easily be directed towards an item of study, a book or a picture, while the latter type comes in wild colours and unusual shapes that delight the eye and create a focal point.

When choosing lighting to work in an old-and-new scheme, ask yourself whether you want a piece that is functional or simply looks good. Either way, there are plenty of styles to choose, from sturdy 1930s desk lights that would look wonderful in a home office to spindly 1950s lamps with conical shades and bold, shapely 1960s lights guaranteed to make an impact wherever they are placed.

Well-known pieces by named designers are very expensive, but it is still possible to find retro examples in smaller antiques shops (and often second-hand office equipment outlets) that are highly affordable. And, of course, some retro-style pieces are still being made today – colourful, quirky lava lamps and groovy, sparkly mirror balls, for example, can be bought in high-street stores; they will give your home an unabashed injection of dazzling and eye-catching kitsch.

OPPOSITE, ABOVE LEFT The 1962 Arco lamp by the Castiglioni brothers has become an icon of modern design. OPPOSITE, BELOW LEFT This utilitarian desk lamp is useful and attractive in a unassuming way. OPPOSITE, RIGHT An early 1950s Italian floor lamp brings character to a minimalist dining area. ABOVE Disco fever comes to a quiet corner of the sitting room in the form of the ever-popular mirrored ball light. RIGHT A bright-red lava lamp adds a quirky touch to a sitting room characterized by clean lines and cool neutrals.

TEXTILES

Whether in the bedroom or the living room, textiles help to create an atmosphere of comfort and cosiness. Vintage textiles, in particular – in the form of curtains, bedspreads, rugs, cushion covers, tablecloths, throws and wall-hangings – will add a sense of homeliness and charm, making even the most modern and minimalist homes feel warm and welcoming.

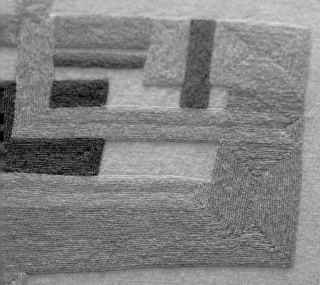

THIS PAGE AND OPPOSITE **Liveliness and interest in this plainest of rooms come from the delicately coloured and patterned bedspread. The softness of fabric contrasts with the hard surfaces of flooring, furniture and architectural detailing.**

FLORAL FABRICS

Using old floral fabrics is a quick way to add prettiness, colour and individuality to a modern room. From delicate sprigs to blowsy blooms, there are patterns suitable for any scheme, in soft pastels or more vivid shades.

In living rooms, use old florals to make curtains or upholstery, if you have enough fabric, or make cushions from smaller pieces. In dining rooms, floral fabrics can be used as tablecloths, runners or napkins, while in bedrooms they work well as pillowcases, bedspreads or quilts.

CLOCKWISE FROM BOTTOM LEFT **Fabric** printed with tiny sprigged flowers on a pale or white background is one of the easiest to use in any room. Floral fabric can be used to cover storage boxes. Seek out lengths of vintage fabric in markets and antique shops – you can hang them on a wall or frame them like paintings. LEFT **Beautiful prints** like these, which are taken from archival patterns, are virtually indistinguishable from their antique counterparts. OPPOSITE **A cosy** floral quilt will be the focal point of any bedroom. Quilts look especially good with painted wooden or metal beds.

UTILITARIAN

In a contemporary home with plain white walls and bare floors, or in a minimal loft full of steel and glass, there is no better way to warm up the space than by adding textiles. Sometimes, however, pretty, chintzy fabrics are not quite appropriate, whereas more practical, utilitarian textiles have the right kind of practical good looks.

The plainest of choices for this type of look is antique linen sheets, washed so many times that they are softer than soft, gorgeous to sleep in or even to use as curtains. Old denim, too, aged by years of use, can be transformed into covers for cushions, seats or small windows. Thick Welsh blankets, in muted colours, are warm and welcoming, whether on a bed or thrown over the back of a sofa, and if you can find examples of old knitting or crochet, they will offer the ultimate in homely, traditional comfort.

All sorts of other old fabrics can be adapted in a similar way, whether bought as lengths in an antiques shop or found in the form of a pair of curtains at a jumble sale. Even old tea towels, shirts or blankets can be cut up and stitched back together, for a casual look that softens the edges of a contemporary room. For this type of old-and-new combination, you should use plains, stripes, ginghams and checks in simple, soft colours – nothing too garish or fussy. But it is possible to create beautiful effects by layering one old fabric on top of another, in harmonizing colours, from pale blue to indigo, or sepia to chocolate, introducing subtle warmth and delicious texture to even the coolest of modern environments.

OPPOSITE **Plump cushions and heavy throws in rich jewel colours bring warmth to an understated modern interior. The textiles add a homely air that softens the clean lines and cool neutrals.**

ABOVE **A traditional check gives a new lease of life to a simple chair seat.**
BELOW **These cushion covers have been made from old linen tea towels. Their soft colours mix beautifully.**

ABSTRACT

To create an interior that makes a strong statement and is more chic than chintzy, abstract textiles are ideal. They will work well anywhere in the home – in the bedroom, the living room, a hallway or a dining room; all rooms, in fact, can benefit from their impact and appeal.

In a contemporary house or flat, retro fabrics coordinate well with a pared-down, clean-lined feel. Without overwhelming a modern scheme, they can inject a note of colour and pattern that provides a pleasant balance or interesting contrast. Fabrics from the 1950s are particularly attractive, with their organic patterns and soft secondary colours. Some examples, such as those designed by Lucienne Day or Marianne Straub for the 1951 Festival of Britain, are hard to come by and command high prices at auction, but it is possible to find less well-known designs in junk shops or jumble sales, often in the form of old curtains or dresses that can be made over into cushion covers, napkins or throws.

There is a wealth of contemporary fabrics available in abstract patterns, in colours that range from neutrals to brights. In a period home they are amazingly effective, counterpointing architectural detailing or antique furniture. Use them as rugs, bedspreads, cushions or curtains, but use them sparingly, since they can be overwhelming in large quantities. Merely one or two pieces will enrich a space with drama and definition.

TOP AND MIDDLE Modern rugs in 1930s-style abstract patterns add a sleek, graphic element to a period interior with ornate architectural features.
BOTTOM The soft colours of this square-printed tablecloth are redolent of 1950s style, and provide a lovely background for plain modern crockery.
OPPOSITE For a unique look with plenty of impact, choose a bedcover printed or woven in retro-style abstracts. Well-defined shapes and strong colours such as these are most effective in a room that is in other respects low-key.

CERAMICS

Both useful and beautiful, ceramics are the ideal accessory.
Whether sleek and modern or intricate and antique, they add
instant personality and warmth, and come in an infinite variety
of styles and colours. Fashionable modern pottery is made in
strong, simple shapes with one-colour glazes, which look
marvellous when contrasted with the architectural detailing of
a traditional home. Old ceramics, on the other hand – chintzy
prints, blue-and-white Delftware or characterful retro pieces –
look particularly effective in a contemporary setting.

OPPOSITE Chintz-printed tea sets are cheap and easy to find. They look particularly effective when displayed in a clean-lined modern kitchen. LEFT A modern unit has been filled with mismatching but delightfully pretty sets of old crockery and other attractive items of kitchenware. BELOW Traditional blue-and-white china has a timeless quality that allows it to fit into any style of home, old or new.

PRETTY & NOSTALGIC

There is nothing more appealing than a delicate bone-china teacup decorated with a chintzy pattern in soft pastels. Inexpensive and easy to come by, these old pieces may not be precious antiques, but they have an old-fashioned charm and friendliness of their own. They can be bought in ones and twos and piled up casually as mismatching sets, either to be used or simply put on display. In a contemporary home, they provide an ideal and unexpected counterpoint to expanses of white-painted wall, wood or stone flooring and the clean, boxy lines of modern furnishings.

For traditionalists who prefer a simpler look, the alternative is the equally delightful and ever-popular blue-and-white china. Willow-pattern china is probably the most familiar, but any second-hand shop is likely have a host of pieces in blue and white, from all sorts of periods and by a range of manufacturers. Choose individual items and sets for their pretty shapes and toning colours, and display them en masse as a fresh, uncontrived addition to a sophisticated contemporary kitchen or dining room.

RETRO

Retro ceramics dating from the period from the 1920s to the 1970s have a unique style that gives the finishing touch to a characterful contemporary room scheme. Since they tend to be rather plain, they harmonize well with modern decoration, but nevertheless they possess a distinctive character, either in their charmingly organic shapes, incised sgraffito decoration or unusual colours, which marks them out as a special choice.

While pieces by important Modernist designers such as Keith Murray would be a rare discovery, there are endless examples of less significant but hugely attractive retro ceramics to be found in junk shops and jumble sales. The key is to pick pieces whose shapes and colours work gracefully together, and to display them in a way that doesn't come across as too cluttered or overpowering.

BELOW AND OPPOSITE, BELOW These simple pieces are by arch-Modernist Keith Murray, and their unadorned forms are typical of his influential 1930s style. They make a marvellous display ranged in a line on a contemporary wood-and-metal sideboard.
OPPOSITE, TOP LEFT Curvy ceramics from the 1950s occupy a set of shelves in an industrial-style loft. OPPOSITE, TOP CENTRE AND RIGHT A 1950s cabinet has become a display area for a set of coffee-coloured ashtrays from the 1960s. The wallpaper framed above them, dating from the 1970s, echoes their colours and shapes.

GLASSWARE

The translucency of glass makes it an ideal decorative element in rooms old or new: subtle and shimmering, it adds elegance and individuality without overpowering other furnishings. Simple forms and subtle colours can be found in glass from all eras, complementing both antique pieces and modern designs. The exceptions are bold, bright pieces from the 1960s, which have an impact and character all their own, and will provide a stunning counterpoint to a room that is otherwise pale and understated.

THIS PAGE AND OPPOSITE **These pieces have in common simple silhouettes and lovely soft colours. They stand out best against a white background, and would work in a pared-down period room or a chic modern setting. Their glossy, hard surfaces would also make a fabulous contrast to textured furnishings such as a suede- or velvet-covered sofa, muslin curtains or a shagpile rug.**

THIS PAGE **To look its best, mid-20th-century glass needs a plain backdrop. If the surroundings are too busy or bright, the pieces will lose their impact.**

RIGHT **This modern Italian glass vase has more than a hint of the 1950s in its joyful colours and sinuous curves.**

RIGHT **These vases in smoky shades are typical of the 1970s. In colour and form; they make a superb counterpoint to period detailing.**
BELOW RIGHT **These bottle vases are wonderful examples of the sheer vivacity and exuberance of mid-20th-century design. Their clear, jewel shades and simple silhouettes are offset perfectly by plain white surroundings.**

COLOURED

Coloured glassware comes in many guises. In an otherwise pale, minimal and understated interior, it offers a wonderful way to add an infusion of vitality, vivacity and a touch of flamboyance.

Pieces from the 1970s in smoky shades have made a comeback as a fashionable accessory, but can still be found in second-hand shops or antiques markets. While subtle in colour, their unusual forms stand out against the clean lines of modern furnishings. Similarly, bold 1960s pieces have a powerful impact in a contemporary home, though they make even more of a statement in a period setting.

Glass made on the Italian island of Murano displays gorgeous colour combinations and complex patterning. These pieces, rare and expensive, are inevitably a focal point in any interior, and combine well with sophisticated but understated furnishings.

Finally, choose contemporary glass to complement a period home. The right colour combinations and simple, flowing lines will resonate quietly in a Georgian or Victorian room.

CLEAR

Clear glass can be used in any style of home to create subtle visual pleasure. While it may be quiet and still, clear glass can nevertheless possess strong character and offer delightful decorative qualities.

Clear antique glassware may be shaped in clear, strong lines – a straight-sided tumbler or a flowing hurricane lamp, for example. Or it may feature delicate fluting or intricate engraving, either abstract or representational. Each type can bring elegance and eclecticism to an avant-garde home or a simple 20th-century interior. A scheme in which intense colours predominate allows clear glass to provide a graceful counterpoint, while in a room decorated with muted neutrals clear glass is a subtle addition.

Retro-style glass tends to feature more decoration, sometimes in the form of quirky, humorous touches. Such pieces can be picked up in junk shops, jumble sales and car-boot sales – but choose carefully to make sure that what you end up with is not just cheap clutter, but a selection that is both intriguing and interesting.

SUPPLIERS

MODERN FURNITURE AND ACCESSORIES

The Conran Shop
81 Fulham Road
London SW3 6RD
020 7589 7401
and branches
www.conran.co.uk
Contemporary furniture, fabrics, lighting and accessories.

Geoffrey Drayton
85 Hampstead Road
London NW1 2PL
020 7387 5840
www.geoffrey-drayton.co.uk
European designer furniture and accessories.

Habitat
0845 6010 740 or
www.habitat.net for branches
Affordable furnishings and accessories.

Heal's
196 Tottenham Court Road
London W1T 7LQ
020 7636 1666
and branches
www.heals.co.uk
Elegant modern design.

Hitch Mylius
Call 020 8443 2616 for
stockists www.hitchmylius.com
Upholstered furniture.

InHouse
28 Howe Street
Edinburgh EH3 6TG
0131 225 2888
and at
24–26 Wilson Street
Glasgow G1 1SS
0141 552 5902
A wide range of contemporary design.

Ligne Roset
Call 0845 602 0267 or
www.ligne-roset.co.uk
for stockists
Interesting modern furniture and lighting.

Lloyd Davies
14 John Dalton Street
Manchester M2 6JR
0161 832 3700
Contemporary pieces.

Loft
Simpsons Fold
24–28 Dock Street
Leeds LS10 1JF
0113 305 1515
www.loftonline.net
Modern designer furniture.

Momentum
31 Charles Street
Cardiff CF10 2GA
029 2023 6266
www.momentumcardiff.com
Four floors of European-designed furniture.

Ocean
Freepost LON 811
London SW18 4BR
0870 848 8480
www.oceancatalogue.com
Mail order catalogue with range of sleek furnishings.

Purves & Purves
220–24 Tottenham Court Road
London W1T 7QE
020 7580 8223
www.purves.co.uk
Colourful, modern furniture and accessories.

Selfridges
400 Oxford Street
London W1A 1AB
020 7629 1234
www.selfridges.co.uk
Contemporary and traditional designs.

ANTIQUES

Bed Bazaar
The Old Station
Station Road, Framlingham
Suffolk IP13 9EE
01728 723756
www.bedbazaar.co.uk
Old beds of all types.

Guinevere
574–80 Kings Road
London SW6 2DY
020 7736 2917
www.guinevere.co.uk
Antiques from ancient to Art Deco, plus fabric, crystal and accessories.

Josephine Ryan Antiques
63 Abbeville Road
London SW4 9JW
020 8675 3900
www.josephineryan
antiques.co.uk
Antique furniture.

Judy Greenwood Antiques
657 Fulham Road
London SW6 5PY
020 7730 6037
www.judygreenwood
antiques.co.uk
French antique pieces.

Pimpernel & Partners
596 Kings Road
London SW6 2DX
020 7731 2448
Good selection of antiques.

MARKETS, SALVAGE AND SECOND-HAND GOODS

Alfie's Antiques Market
13–25 Church Street
London NW8 8DT
Wide range of stalls.

Andy Thornton Architectural Antiques
Victoria Mills
Stainland Road
Greetland, Halifax
West Yorkshire HX4 8AD
01422 377314
www.andythornton.com
Huge warehouse.

Au Temps Perdu
30 Midland Road
St Phillips
Bristol BS2 0JY
0117 955 9143
www.autempsperdu.co.uk
General salvage.

Castle Gibson
106a Upper Street
London N1 12N
020 7704 0927
www.castlegibson.com
Upmarket reconditioned office furniture, from plan chests to filing cabinets.

Drummonds
The Kirkpatrick Buildings
25 London Road
Hindhead
Surrey GU26 6AB
01428 609444
www.drummonds-arch.co.uk
Extensive range.

The Ginnel Gallery
Lloyds House
Manchester M2 5WA
0161 833 9037
Antiques and retro centre.

LASSCo
St Michael's Church
Mark Street
London EC2A 4ER
020 7739 0448
www.lassco.co.uk
Architectural salvage in a Victorian church.

Pew Corner
Artington Manor Farm
Old Portsmouth Road
Guildford
Surrey GU3 1LP
01483 533337
Reclaimed ecclesiastical and other pieces.

Salvo
www.salvo.co.uk
Lists of authorized reclamation dealers around the country and in France.

Solopark
Station Road
Pampisford
Cambridgeshire CB2 4HB
01223 834663
www.solopark.co.uk
*Vast range on a
2.5 hectare site.*

Walcot Reclamation
108 Walcot Street
Bath BA1 5BG
01225 44404
www.walcot.com
*Architectural antiques plus
traditional building materials.*

MID-20TH CENTURY
AND RETRO STYLE

Aero
347–49 Kings Road
London SW3 5ES
020 7351 0511
info@aerobydesign.com
Classic designer furniture.

After Noah
121 Upper Street
London N1 1QP
020 7359 4281
and at
261 Kings Road
London SW3 5EL
020 7351 2610
www.afternoah.com
*Pieces from the 1930s
and 1940s.*

Anglepoise
Call 01527 63771 for stockists
The classic 1930s lamps.

Aram
110 Drury Lane
London WC2B 5SG
020 7557 7557
aramstore@aram.co.uk
*Modern furniture, lighting and
accessories from new and
established designers.*

Best & Lloyd
Call 0121 558 1191
for stockists
*1930s floor, wall-mounted
and table 'Bestlite', still in
production.*

Boom Interiors
115–17 Regents Park Road
London NW1 8UR
020 7722 6622
www.boominteriors.com
*Original 20th-century furniture,
lighting and accessories.*

Cath Kidston
8 Clarendon Cross
London W11 4AP
020 7221 4000
and stockists
www.cathkidston.co.uk
*Pretty accessories and fabric
with a retro feel.*

Eatmyhandbagbitch
6 Dray Walk
The Old Truman Brewery
91–95 Brick Lane
London E1 6RL
020 7375 3100
A range of vintage pieces.

Flying Duck Enterprises
320–22 Creek Road
London SE10 9SW
020 8858 1964
www.flying-duck.com
*Designs from the 1950s
to the 1970s.*

Target Gallery
7 Windmill Street
London W1P 1HF
020 7636 6295
*Mainly post-war furniture
and tableware.*

Twentytwentyone
274 Upper Street
London N1 2UA
020 7288 1996
*Original pieces by important
designers.*

SYMPATHETIC
REPRODUCTIONS

Bennison Fabrics
Call 020 7730 8076 for
stockists
www.bennisonfabrics.com
*Florals from 18th- and
19th-century designs.*

Grand Illusions
41 Crown Road
St Margarets
Middlesex TW1 3EJ
020 8607 9446 or
01747 854092 for mail order
www.grandillusions.co.uk
Pretty furniture.

Laura Ashley
Call 0870 5622116 for
branches or
0800 868100 for mail order
www.lauraashley.com
*Pretty, traditional-style fabrics,
furniture and accessories.*

Scumble Goosie
Lewiston Mill
Toadsmoor Road
Brimscombe, Stroud
Gloucestershire GL5 2TB
01453 731305
www.scumble-goosie.co.uk
*French and Gustavian-style
furniture in MDF, ready to be
painted.*

SHOPS THAT SELL BOTH
OLD AND NEW

Babylon
301 Fulham Road
London SW10 9QH
020 7376 7235
*Contemporary lighting and
accessories, with antique
furniture.*

English Country Living
The Chapel
Chapel Lane, Caythorpe
Nr Grantham
Lincolnshire NG32 3EG
01400 273632
*Antiques, painted furniture,
sofas, chairs, mirrors, lighting,
fabrics, wallpaper, paint.*

Interiors Bis
60 Sloane Avenue
London SW3 3DD
020 7838 1104
www.interiorsbis.com
*Contemporary furniture, lighting
and rugs, plus pieces that
date from the 19th century to
the 1940s.*

Nicholas Haslam
12 Holbein Place
London SW1W 8NL
020 7730 8623
www.nicholashaslam.com
*Furniture and accessories, both
antique and modern.*

Ogier
177 Westbourne Grove
London W11 2SB
020 7229 0783
*Antique Asian furniture, plus
contemporary furniture and
lighting.*

Sieff
49 Long Street
Tetbury
Gloucestershire GL8 8AA
01666 504477
www.sieff.co.uk
*Mixture of furniture and
accessories from the
18th to the 21st centuries.*

Skandium
86 Marylebone High Street
London W1U 4QS
245–49 Brompton Road
London SW3 2EP
020 7935 2077
www.skandium.com
*Scandinavian design classics
and modern designs.*

Story
Call 020 7377 0313
for an appointment
*Furniture and accessories
selected by a former stylist.*

Valerie Wade
108 Fulham Road
London SW3 6HS
020 7225 1414
www.valeriewade.com
*Art Deco pieces, together with
new chrome lighting and silver
bedroom furniture.*

William Yeoward
270 Kings Road
London SW3 5AW
020 7349 7828
www.williamyeoward.com
*Eclectic mixture of old and
new pieces.*

PICTURE CREDITS

KEY ph=photographer; a=above, b=below, r=right, l=left, c=centre.

1 ph Polly Wreford/Adria Ellis's apartment in
New York; **2–3** ph Tom Leighton/Keith Varty
& Alan Cleaver's apartment in London,
designed by Jonathan Reed (Studio Reed);
4l ph Polly Wreford/Daniel Jasiak's
apartment in Paris; **4r** ph Polly Wreford/
Ann Shore's house in London; **5** ph Polly
Wreford/Glenn Carwithen & Sue Miller's
house in London, painting by Alan
Grimwood; **6** ph Tom Leighton; **8–9** ph
Tom Leighton; **10–11** ph Polly Wreford/
Glenn Carwithen & Sue Miller's house in
London; **12 & 13b** ph Tom Leighton; **13a** ph
Ray Main/client's residence, East Hampton,
New York, designed by ZG DESIGN; **14a**
ph Polly Wreford/Lena Proudlock's house
in Gloucestershire; **14b** ph Chris Everard/
interior designer Ann Boyd's own apartment
in London; **15** ph Polly Wreford/The
Sawmills Studios; **16–17** ph Tom Leighton;
17 ph Chris Everard/François Muracciole's
apartment in Paris; **18** ph Ray Main/
Gisela Garson's house in Stoke Newington,
designed by FAT; **18–19** ph Ray Main/David
Mellor's home and studio at Hathersage in
Derbyshire; **20l** both ph Alan Williams/Katie
Bassford King's house in London, designed
by Touch Interior Design; **20r** ph Polly
Wreford/Clare Nash's house in London; **21**
ph Verity Welstead/Lulu Guinness's house in
London; **22, 23l & 23ar** ph Andrew Wood/
Norma Holland's house in London; **23br**
ph Polly Wreford/Ros Fairman's house in
London; **24al** ph Polly Wreford/an apartment
in New York, designed by Belmont Freeman
Architects; **24–25a** ph Ray Main/Evan
Snyderman's house in Brooklyn; **24b** ph
Polly Wreford/home of 27.12 Design Ltd,
Chelsea, NYC; **26** ph Tom Leighton/interior
designer Philip Hooper's own house in East
Sussex; **27** ph Ray Main/Thierry Watorek's
house near Paris; **28–29** ph Ray Main/
Greville & Sophie Worthington's home in
Yorkshire; **30a** both ph Andrew Wood/
Roger & Fay Oates's house in Eastnor,
Herefordshire; **30br** ph Catherine Gratwicke/
Intérieurs in New York; **31** ph Catherine
Gratwicke/an apartment in Paris, designed
by Bruno Tanquerel; **32** ph Polly Wreford;
33al ph Tom Leighton; **33ar** ph Catherine
Gratwicke/Martin Barrell & Amanda Sellers's
flat, owners of Maisonette, London; **33bl**

ph Polly Wreford/Kathy Moskal's apartment
in New York, designed by Ken Foreman;
33cl & br ph Tom Leighton;**34ar & br** ph
Polly Wreford/an apartment in New York,
designed by Belmont Freeman Architects;
34ar ph Tom Leighton; **34br** ph Catherine
Gratwicke/Frances Robinson & Eamonn
McMahon's house in London; **35** ph Thomas
Stewart/The T House in London, designed
by Ian Chee of VX Design; **36** ph James
Merrell; **37** ph Andrew Wood/Norma
Holland's house in London; **38al** ph Ray
Main/Marie-Pierre Morel's house in Paris,
designed by François Muracciole; **38bl** ph
Chris Everard/Eric De Queker's apartment
in Antwerp; **38–39** ph Ray Main/Kenneth
Hirst's apartment in New York; **39** ph Polly
Wreford/Carol Reid's apartment in Paris;
40l ph Chris Everard/François Muracciole's
apartment in Paris; **40r & 41** ph James
Merrell/Christine Walsh & Ian Bartlett's
house in London, designed by Jack Ingham
of Bookworks; **42** ph Polly Wreford/Ros
Fairman's house in London; **43al** ph Alan
Williams/interior designer and managing
director of the Société Yves Halard, Michelle
Halard's own apartment in Paris; **43ar** ph
Polly Wreford/The Sawmills Studios; **43bl**
ph Chris Everard/François Muracciole's
apartment in Paris; **44a** ph Tom Leighton;
44b ph Tom Leighton/paint Farrow & Ball:
floor Mouse's Back floor paint no. 40,
cupboards Green Smoke no. 47 and interior
Red Fox no. 48, walls and woodwork String
no. 8, ceiling Off White no. 3; **45** ph James
Merrell/Sally Butler's house in London; **46** ph
James Merrell/Ash Sakula's house in London;
47a ph James Merrell/Stephen Woodhams's
house in London, designed in conjunction
with Mark Brook Design; **47b** ph James
Merrell/John Alexander & Fiona Waterstreet's
loft in New York, designed by Lorraine Kirke;
48al ph Catherine Gratwicke/Lulu Guinness's
home in London; **48bl** ph Verity Welstead/
Lulu Guinness's house in London; **48r & 49**
ph Catherine Gratwicke/Agnès Emery's
house in Brussels: tiles, star light and drawer
handles from Emery & Cie; **50** ph Catherine
Gratwicke/Etienne & Mary Millner's house in
London, ceramics from Selfridges; **51al & bl**
ph Catherine Gratwicke; **51r** ph Catherine
Gratwicke/The Jeff McKay Inc. advertising

and public relations agency in New York,
designed by David Mann & James Corbett;
52 ph Andrew Wood; **53** ph Chris Everard/
an apartment in London, designed by Jo
Hagan of USE Architects; **54l & 55l** ph Tom
Leighton/a loft in London, designed by
Robert Dye Associates, chairs Twentieth
Century Design, wooden containers David
Wainwright, bamboo plates, bowl and
ceramic bowls David Champion; **54r** ph
Andrew Wood/Norma Holland's house in
London; **55r** ph Andrew Wood/Chelsea loft
apartment in New York, designed by The
Moderns; **56** ph Polly Wreford/The Sawmills
Studios; **57cl** ph James Merrell/John
Alexander & Fiona Waterstreet's loft in New
York designed by Lorraine Kirke; **57al** ph
James Merrell/Ash Sakula's house in London;
57ar ph Polly Wreford/Glenn Carwithen &
Sue Miller's house in London; **57b** both ph
Andrew Wood/the home of Gwen Aldridge
& Bruce McLucas; **58al** ph Verity Welstead/
Lulu Guinness's house in London; **58ar** ph
Andrew Wood/the Pasadena, California,
home of Susan D'Avignon; **58bl** ph Ray Main/
Thierry Watorek's house near Paris; **58br** ph
Andrew Wood/media executive's house in
Los Angeles, architect: Stephen Slan, builder:
Ken Duran, furnishings: Russell Simpson,
original architect: Carl Maston c.1945; **59**
ph Andrew Wood/Norma Holland's house
in London; **60–61** ph Alan Williams/Katie
Bassford King's house in London, designed
by Touch Interior Design; **62** ph Polly Wreford/
Adria Ellis's apartment in New York, painting
by Peter Zangrillo; **63al** ph Henry Bourne;
63bl ph Andrew Wood/John Cheim's
apartment in New York; **63r** ph Tom Leighton;
64l ph Tom Leighton; **64r** ph Polly Wreford/
Lena Proudlock's house in Gloucestershire;
65 ph Polly Wreford/The Sawmills Studios;
66 ph Polly Wreford/Carol Reid's apartment
in Paris; **67** ph Tom Leighton; **68a & c**
ph Polly Wreford/Ros Fairman's house in
London; **68b** ph Catherine Gratwicke;
69 ph Polly Wreford/Mary Foley's house in
Connecticut; **70 & 71a** ph Andrew Wood/
media executive's house in Los Angeles,
architect: Stephen Slan, builder: Ken Duran,
furnishings: Russell Simpson, original
architect: Carl Maston c.1945; **71b** ph
Andrew Wood/Kurt Bredenbeck's apartment

at the Barbican, London; **72** ph Catherine Gratwicke/the brownstone in New York of Bonnie Young, director of global sourcing and inspiration at Donna Karan International; **73** ph Tom Leighton/Keith Varty & Alan Cleaver's apartment in London, designed by Jonathan Reed (Studio Reed); **74** ph Henry Bourne; **75al** ph Alan Williams/the architect Voon Wong's own apartment in London; **75ar** ph Polly Wreford/Ros Fairman's house in London; **75bl** ph Polly Wreford/home of 27.12 Design Ltd, Chelsea, NYC; **75br** ph Andrew Wood/Heidi Kingstone's apartment in London; **76al & br** ph Polly Wreford; **76ar** ph Polly Wreford/Clare Nash's house in London; **76bl** ph Polly Wreford/Ros Fairman's house in London; **77** ph Alan Williams/owner of Gloss, Pascale Bredillet's own apartment in London; **78–79** ph Andrew Wood/Alastair Hendy & John Clinch's apartment in London, designed by Alastair Hendy; **80 & 81al** ph Alan Williams/Katie Bassford King's house in London, designed by Touch Interior Design; **81ar** ph Catherine Gratwicke/Ellis Flyte's house in London; **81br** ph Ray Main/Kirk & Caroline Pickering's house in London, space creation by Square Foot Properties Ltd; **82al & r** ph Andrew Wood/a house in London, designed by Bowles & Linares; **82bl** ph Andrew Wood/Alastair Hendy & John Clinch's apartment in London, designed by Alastair Hendy; **83** ph Polly Wreford/Kathy Moskal's apartment in New York, designed by Ken Foreman; **84** ph Ray Main/Jonathan Leitersdorf's apartment in New York, designed by Jonathan Leitersdorf/Just Design Ltd; **85l** ph Catherine Gratwicke/the brownstone in New York of Bonnie Young, director of global sourcing and inspiration at Donna Karan International; **85ar** ph Chris Everard/an apartment in Milan, designed by Nicoletta Marazza; **85br** ph Chris Everard/ Sera Hersham-Loftus' house in London; **86al** ph Chris Everard/Gentucca Bini's apartment in Milan; **86r** ph Chris Everard/ Lulu Guinness's house in London; **86bl** ph Chris Everard/Florence Buchanan, Steve Harrison & Octavia Spelman's house, Tribeca, New York, designed by Sage Wimer Coombe Architects; **87** ph Polly Wreford/ Ros Fairman's house in London; **88–89** ph Ray Main/Marina & Peter Hill's barn in West Sussex, designed by Marina Hill, Peter James Construction Management, Chichester, The West Sussex Antique Timber Company, Wisborough Green, and Joanna Jefferson Architects; **90** both ph Chris Everard/Mark Kirkley & Harumi

Kaijima's house in Sussex; **91** ph Tom Leighton/Roger & Fay Oates's house in Eastnor, Herefordshire; **92** ph Andrew Wood/a house in London designed by Bowles & Linares; **93al & br** ph Chris Everard/ Sera Hersham-Loftus' house in London; **93ar & bl** ph Chris Everard/ Suzanne Slesin & Michael Steinberg's apartment in New York, design by Jean-Louis Ménard; **94–95** ph Alan Williams/ owner of Gloss, Pascale Bredillet's own apartment in London; **96–97** ph Polly Wreford/Daniel Jasiak's apartment in Paris; **98l** ph Ray Main/Evan Snyderman's house in Brooklyn; **98ar** ph Tom Leighton; **98br** ph Verity Welstead/Alison & Paul Holberton's house in Southwark, London; **99a** ph Andrew Wood/Mary Shaw's Sequana apartment in Paris; **99b** ph James Merrell; **100** ph Andrew Wood/Neil Bingham's house in Blackheath, London, chair from Designer's Guild; **101a** ph Andrew Wood/Ian Chee's apartment in London, chair courtesy of Vitra; **101bl** ph Andrew Wood/Brian Johnson's apartment in London, designed by Johnson Naylor, chairs courtesy of Race Furniture; **101br** ph Tom Leighton/interior designer Philip Hooper's own house in East Sussex; **102–103** all ph Tom Leighton; **104** ph Andrew Wood/Ian Bartlett & Christine Walsh's house in London; **105l** ph Andrew Wood; **105r** ph Tom Leighton; **106** ph Andrew Wood/a house in London, designed by Guy Stansfeld (020 7727 0133); **107al** ph Tom Leighton; **107b** ph Andrew Wood/the London flat of Miles Johnson & Frank Ronan; **107r** ph Andrew Wood; **108a** ph Catherine Gratwicke/Kimball Mayer & Meghan Hughes's apartment in New York, designed by L.A. Morgan; **108bl** ph Polly Wreford/ home of 27.12 Design Ltd, Chelsea, NYC; **108br** ph Polly Wreford/an apartment in New York, designed by Belmont Freeman Architects; **109** ph Catherine Gratwicke/ Sean & Mary Kelly's loft in New York, designed by Steven Learner; **110 &111al** ph Tom Leighton; **111ar** ph Catherine Gratwicke/Johanne Riss's house in Brussels; **111br** ph Tom Leighton/paint Paint Library, chair fabric Livingstone Studio, lamp Valerie Wade, artwork by Zoë Hope, table Josephine Ryan; **112–13** ph Alan Williams/Géraldine Prieur's apartment in Paris, an interior designer fascinated with colour; **114l** both ph Andrew Wood/Phillip Low, New York; **115l** ph Polly Wreford/Ann Shore's house in London; **115ar** ph Polly Wreford; **115br** ph Fritz von der Schulenburg; **116al** ph Andrew Wood;

116bl ph Polly Wreford; **116r & 117a** ph Andrew Wood/Guido Palau's house in north London, designed by Azman Owens Architects; **117b** ph Chris Everard/Reuben Barrett's apartment in London, light from Mathmos; **118–19** ph Andrew Wood/Chelsea loft apartment in New York, designed by The Moderns; **120al, ar & br** all ph Polly Wreford; **120br** ph Verity Welstead; **121** ph Tom Leighton; **122** ph Andrew Wood/Mary Shaw's Sequana apartment in Paris; **123** both ph James Merrell; **124al** ph Andrew Wood/Chelsea loft apartment in New York, designed by The Moderns; **124c** ph Andrew Wood/Jane Collins of Sixty 6 in Marylebone High Street, home in central London; **124b** ph Polly Wreford; **125** ph Andrew Wood/Jo Shane, John Cooper & family, apartment in New York; **126–27** ph Polly Wreford/home of 27.12 Design Ltd, Chelsea, NYC; **128 & 129l** ph Polly Wreford/Clare Nash's house in London; **129br** ph Chris Everard; **130 & 131b** ph Alan Williams/director of design consultants Graven Images, Janice Kirkpatrick's apartment in Glasgow; **131al** ph Catherine Gratwicke/Kari Sigerson's apartment in New York; **131ac & ar** ph Tom Leighton; **132** ph Tham Nhu-Tran; **133** ph Polly Wreford; **134** ph Polly Wreford; **135al** ph Polly Wreford/Clare Nash's house in London; **135ar** ph Catherine Gratwicke/ Martin Barrell & Amanda Sellers's flat, owners of Maisonette, London; **135br** ph Tham Nhu-Tran/Ian Chee's house in London; **136l** ph David Brittain; **136r** ph Tom Leighton; **137l** ph Tom Leighton/Roger & Fay Oates's house in Eastnor, Herefordshire; **137r** both ph Tom Leighton.

ACKNOWLEDGMENTS

Publisher's acknowledgments: In addition to the designers, architects and home owners mentioned above, the publishers would also like to thank Netty Nauta, Aleid Rontgen and Annette Brederode, designers Roxanne Beis and Jean-Bernard Navier, Caroline and Michael Breet, Marilyn Phipps, Shiraz Maneksha, Glen Senk and Brian Johnson of Anthropologie, Tricia Foley, George Laaland at Woolloomooloo Restaurant, Potted Gardens and Angela Miller & Russell Glover.

Author's acknowledgments: I'd like to thank my family, friends and colleagues for their constant and unstinting support, advice and help while I was writing this book.

BUSINESS CREDITS

KEY a=above, b=below, r=right, l=left, c=centre.

27.12 Design Ltd
333 Hudson Street, 10th Floor
New York, NY 10014
USA
+ 1 212 727 8169
www.2712design.com
Pages 24b, 75bl, 108bl, 126–27.

Alastair Hendy
Food writer, art director
and designer
f. 020 7739 6040
Pages 78–79, 82bl.

Ann Boyd Design
Studio 8, Fairbank Studios
Lots Road
London SW10 ONS
020 7351 4098
Page 14b.

Ann Shore
(by appointment only)
Story
020 7377 0313
Pages 4r, 115l.

Annette Brederode
(by appointment only)
Lynbaansgracht 56d
Amsterdam
The Netherlands
Pages 8–9, 102–103a.

Anthropologie
www.anthropologie.com
Pages 63r, 107bl.

Ash Sakula Architects
24 Rosebery Avenue
London EC1R 4SX
020 7837 9735
www.ashsak.com
Pages 46, 57cl.

Azman Associates
(formerly Azman Owens
Architects)
18 Charlotte Road
London EC2A 3PB
020 7739 8191
www.azmanarchitects.com
Pages 116r, 117a.

**Belmont Freeman
Architects**
project team:
Belmont Freeman (principal
designer), Alane Truitt
Sangho Park
110 West 40th Street
New York, NY 10018
USA
+ 1 212 382 3311
Pages 24al, 34ar, 34br, 108br.

Bonnie Young
Director of global sourcing
and inspiration at
Donna Karan International
+ 1 212 228 0832
Pages 72, 85l.

Bowles & Linares
32 Hereford Road
London W2 5AJ
020 7229 9886
www.bowlesandlinares.co.uk
Pages 82al, 82r, 92.

Bruno Tanquerel, Artist
2 passage St. Sébastien
75011 Paris
France
+ 33 1 43 57 03 93
Page 31.

Caroline Breet
Caroline's Antiek & Brocante
Nieuweweg 35A
251 LH Laren
The Netherlands
Pages 16–17.

Daniel Jasiak, Designer
12 rue Jean Ferrandi
Paris 75006
France
+ 33 1 45 49 13 56
Pages 4l, 96–97.

David Mann
MR Architecture + Décor
150 West 28th Street, 1102
New York, NY 10001
USA
+ 1 212 989 9300

mann@mrarch.com
James Corbett can
be contacted through
David Mann.
Page 51r.

David Mellor Design
Hathersage
Sheffield S32 1BA
01433 650 220
davidmellor@ukonline.co.uk
Pages 18–19.

Ellis Flyte
Fashion designer
f. 020 7431 7560
Page 81ar.

**Emery & Cie and Noir
D'Ivorie**
27 rue de l'Hôpital
Brussels
Belgium
+ 32 2 513 5892
www.emeryetcie.com
Pages 48r, 49.

Eric De Queker
DQ Design In Motion
Koninklijkelaan 44
2600 Bercham
Belgium
Page 38bl.

Farrow & Ball
www.farrow-ball.com
Page 44b.

FAT
Appletree Cottage
116–20 Golden Lane
London EC1Y OTL
020 7251 6735
www.fat.co.uk
Page 18.

Frances Robinson
Detail jewellery designers
and consultants
020 7582 9564
Page 34br.

François Muracciole
Architect
54 rue de Montreuil
75011 Paris
France
+ 33 1 43 71 33 03
francois.muracciole@libertysurf.fr
Pages 17, 38al, 40l, 43bl.

Géraldine Prieur
Interior designer
2 Boulevard Pershing
75017 Paris
France
+ 33 6 11 19 42 86
www.geraldineprieur.com
Pages 112, 113.

Gloss
Home accessories
274 Portobello Road
London W10 5TE
020 8960 4146
pascale@glossltd.u-net.com
Pages 77, 94–95.

Hirst Pacific
250 Lafayette Street
New York, NY 10012
USA
+ 1 212 625 3670
www.hirstpacific.com
Pages 38–39.

Intérieurs
114 Wooster Street
New York, NY 10012
USA
Page 30br.

Jack Ingham
Bookworks
34 Ansleigh Place
London W11 4BW
020 7792 8310
Pages 40r, 41.

Jean-Louis Ménard
32 boulevard de l'Hôpital
75005 Paris
France
+ 33 43 36 31 74
Pages 93ar, 93l.